MW00810693

GEORGE WASHINGTON

and

WINCHESTER, VIRGINIA

1748 - 1758

*A Decade of Preparation
for Responsibilities to Come*

By

GARLAND R. QUARLES

Volume VIII: Winchester - Frederick County
Historical Society Papers

International Standard Book Number
0-923198-01-6

SECOND PRINTING
1989

PRINTED IN THE UNITED STATES OF AMERICA

Printed by
COMMERCIAL PRESS, INC.
Stephens City, VA 22655

Courtesy — Washington and Lee University

GEORGE WASHINGTON AND WINCHESTER, VIRGINIA

1748 - 1758

A Decade of Preparation for Responsibilities to Come

George Washington first viewed the site of Winchester on March 16, 1748 (*Diary* I - Page 6). It was then called Frederick Town and was the County seat of the recently created County of Frederick. Washington at that time had just passed his sixteenth birthday and certainly had no reason then to anticipate how many days during the next ten years he was to spend in this little frontier town, nor of how much the experiences of those ten years were to contribute to his training for command in the larger area to which he was to be called later. He came to Winchester as a boy in 1748; he left Winchester in 1758 as a seasoned leader of men, who had known defeat, debilitating illness, the intrigues of army life, the frustrations of inadequate support, here and there a measure of limited success, the mortal dangers of battle, and all the other irritations and uncertainties which he was later to experience as Commander-in-Chief of the American forces during the Revolution. Yes, Washington from his headquarters at Winchester was schooled in the rough classroom of frontier warfare to lead America to her independence.

Washington was in Winchester in 1748 as one of a surveying party sent out by William Fairfax, cousin and agent of Thomas Lord Fairfax, Proprietor of the Northern Neck of Virginia. This statement requires that we should clarify by explanation the

Washington-Fairfax relationship. In 1748 George Washington was spending much of his time at Mt. Vernon, the home of his half-brother Lawrence Washington. A few miles down the Potomac from *Mt. Vernon* was *Belvoir* the estate of William Fairfax. Lawrence had married Ann, the eldest daughter of William Fairfax. There was constant intercourse between the two households, and George developed a strong attachment for William Fairfax; and this regard seems to have been reciprocated by the older man if we are to judge by the expressions of esteem and genuine affection contained in Fairfax's letters to the youthful Washington.

William Fairfax was a man of real distinction and influence in the Colony of Virginia. He was the son of Henry Fairfax of Yorkshire, England and grandson of Thomas the Fourth Lord Fairfax. At the age of twenty-one he entered the British army, serving in Spain and the East Indies. He took part in the expedition against Providence Island and its pirate rulers and was appointed governor of the island and later as Chief Justice of the Bahama Islands, but since the climate of that region did not agree with him, he moved to New England for a short period. Later Lord Fairfax induced him to become manager of his huge Northern Neck Proprietary, and William came to Virginia where he established himself at Belvoir. Here he died September 3, 1757.

William Fairfax was married twice: first to Sarah Walker, to which union were born George William, Thomas, Anne, and Sarah; second to Debora Clarke by whom he had three children: Bryan, William, and Hannah. Thomas was an officer in the Royal Navy and was killed in the East Indies in 1746. Anne, the eldest daughter, as we have previously indicated, was married first to Lawrence Washington and after his death to George Lee. Sarah married John Carlyle, the well known merchant and business man of Alexandria. Bryan, who was to become the 8th Lord Fairfax, lived in Fairfax County. William, the fourth son, was killed in the famous siege of Quebec.

George William Fairfax, the oldest child, was educated in England. He married the daughter of Col. Cary of Hampton. He was a Burgess from Frederick County and succeeded his father William as Lord Fairfax's agent in 1757. He returned to England in 1773 and never came back to Virginia. He died at Bath April 3, 1787. George William was born in 1752 and was, therefore, seven years George Washington's senior.

Belvoir the William Fairfax home was destroyed by fire after it passed out of the hands of the Fairfax family. Today the ruins of the home and the Fairfax graveyard are in almost the center of the United States Army installation Fort Belvoir.

On March 11, 1748 George William Fairfax and young George Washington, together with several others left *Belvoir* for the Shenandoah Valley to complete some surveys for Lord Fairfax. They traveled south to Dumfries, it is thought, and then turned west on an ancient road leading to Ashby's Bent or Gap over the Blue Ridge Mountains. They stopped for the night at the inn of George Neavil which stood in what is today the Village of Auburn in Fauquier County. Here they were joined by James Genn. who was the County Surveyor of Prince William County and who had completed many surveys for Lord Fairfax in the Northern Neck. The details of this expedition are set forth in the first of Washington's many diaries which he entitled "A Journal of My Journey over the Mountains."

The party proceeded over the Blue Ridge at Ashby's Gap, probably crossed the Shenandoah by Capt John Ashby's ferry, and turned southward to the "Quarters" of Lord Fairfax, Greenway Court, his well known seat, not having been built until a year later. They spent Sunday, March 13 with Lord Fairfax. On the next day, March 14, then sent their baggage to Yost Hite's who lived and ran an inn at present-day Bartonsville, and the surveying party went about 16 miles down the Shenandoah to Capt. Isaac Pennington's "in order to lay off some lands on Cates Marsh and Long Marsh." (*Diaries* Vol. I - Page 5.) Cates Marsh and Long Marsh are small streams in present-day Jefferson County, West Virginia in the vicinity of Charles Town in what is often referred to as the "Bull Skin" creek area.

Two days later (March 16) we find this entry in the Diary.

"We set out early and finish'd about one oclock and then Travell'd up to Frederick Town where our baggage

3

came to us we cleaned ourselves (to get rid of Y. Game we had catched the Night before) and took a Review of Y. town and thence return'd to our Lodgings where we had a good Dinner prepared for us Wine and Rum Punch in Plenty and a good feather bed with Clean sheets which was a very agreeable regale." (*Diaries* Vol. I - Page 6)

So on this day, March 16, 1748, as we have previously indicated, George Washington "took a review" of the site of the town of Winchester for the first time, and spent his first night there in one of her inns. Just what did young Washington see when he took his "review" on that memorable evening? Ten years before in 1738 according to Kercheval (Page 175) the place consisted of only two cabins on the town run. That same year the County of Frederick had been authorized by the Virginia House of Burgesses, but it was not until 1744 that the real organization of the County had been effected. The first Court had met in 1744 at the home of James Wood, called *Glen Burnie,* located near a fine limestone spring, the source of the Town Run. On March 9 of the same year James Wood, who had been made Clerk of the Court of the newly-formed County, laid off on his land twenty-six numbered half acre lots and four unnumbered lots, the former of which were to house the inhabitants of the newly selected county seat and the latter to be the sites of its public buildings. By 1748 a court house, a jail, and a chapel of the established church had been erected on these public lots. Brother Gottlieb, a minister of the Moravian church passed through Winchester in October 1753 and reported in his journal that there were "about 60 houses, which are rather poorly built." (*Va. Mag. of Hist. & Biog.,* Vol. 12 - Page 142). This is the town approximately as Washington saw it his first time. It was then called Frederick Town, but four years later in 1752, when it received its formal charter by the House of Burgesses, it was named Winchester.

On Thursday, March 17, the surveying party set out for the South Branch of the Potomac, their original destination. They avoided a direct route westward from Winchester because in that direction were continuous mountains and no road. They chose rather a roundabout journey. First they traveled north to the Potomac. Finding it swollen by rains so as to prevent fording, they passed the time visiting Bath, Frederick Springs or now Berkeley Springs. Later when the water in the Potomac had to some degree subsided they swam the horses across and carried their equipment across in canoes to the Maryland side of the river. They then proceeded up river to Cresap's Plantation (Present-day Oldtown, Md.), which is on the north branch just above the junction of the north and south branches of the Potomac. They then recrossed the river (now the north branch) and made their way to the region on the South Branch lying between present-day Romney and Petersburg, West Virginia. In this area they remained until April 11, surveying daily. On several occasions Surveyor Genn permitted young Washington to handle the transit and direct the operation, invaluable experience for the young man soon to become a surveyor in his own right.

On April 11 Washington and George William Fairfax rode down to Frederick Town by way of "Coddy's" (*Diaries* Vol 1 - P. 12), the forks of Capon, and the Bloomery Gap. They dined in town and lodged at Hite's. The next day they set out for home, Washington reaching Mt. Vernon on April 13. Thus ended his first contact with the Virginia frontier.

George's interest in surveying had developed before he had his extensive experience with it in the wilds of western Frederick County. His father had practiced surveying, and young Washington had experimented with his parent's instruments at an early age. On his return from "over the mountains" he appears to have resolved to become a registered, officially licensed surveyor He must have obtained instruction from some source in his preparation for the official examination that he had to pass to become a surveyor, but there are no records to show who gave it. However, regardless of the obstacles he had to surmount, the records of Culpeper County show that on July 31, 1749 the "Masters of the College of William and Mary" approved the qualifications and authorized him to enter into the business of surveying. In the fall of that same year he received an invitation from Lord Fairfax to meet the Proprietor in Frederick at the November term of the Court with the promise that his lordship would engage him to make surveys for him. (*Writings of Washington* Vol. I - Page 18). For the next four years Washington worked for the proprietor of the Northern Neck usually in the early spring and late fall. Specifically his Survey Field Book seems to indicate that he was surveying in old Frederick County during the following approximate periods: (Note: Old Frederick County included the modern Virginia counties of Frederick, Clarke, Shenandoah, Warren and part of Page; and the West Virginia Counties of Jefferson, Berkeley, Morgan, Hampshire, part of Hardy and parts of several other West Virginia Counties.)

November 2, 1749 to November 11, 1749

March 30, 1750 to April 28, 1750

October 11, 1750 to October 24, 1750

March 26, 1751 - Made a few surveys around this date

March 19, 1752 to May 1, 1752

The survey book indicates that during this period of time Washington completed surveys on the Capon River, the South Branch of the Potomac, Dillon's Run, the Little Cacapon River, the Bullskin Creek, and a few other locations. The book lists a very few surveys in present-day Frederick County or in areas close to Winchester. The question arises as to how much of his time Washington spent in Winchester (then Frederick Town) during his surveying experience from 1749 to 1752. In a letter directed to "Richard" and written according to Dr. Freeman about Nov. 8, 1749 (*Freeman* I - 238) (*G.W.* - I - Pages 17) he says.

"Dear Richard: The receipt of your kind favor of the 2nd of this instant afforded me unspeakable pleasure as I am convinced that I am still in the Memory of so Worthy a friend a friendship I shall ever be proud of Increasing you gave me the more pleasure as I receiv'd it amongst a parcel of Barbarians and an uncooth set of People the like favor often repeated would give me pleasure although I seem to be in a Place where no real Satis: be had since you receid my letter in October Last. I have not sleeped above three nights or Four in a bed but after walking a good deal all the day lay down before the fire upon a little Hay Straw Fodder or bairskin whichever is to be had with man wife and Children like a Parcel of Dogs or Catts and happy's he that gets the birth nearest the Fire theres nothing would make it pass off tolerably but a good reward a Dubloon is my constant gain every day that the weather will permit my going out and sometime Six Pistoles the coldness of the weather will not allow my making a long stay us the Lodging is rather too cold for the time of year I have never had my cloths off but lay and sleep in them

6

like a negro except the few nights I have lay'n in **Frederick Town.**"

This letter would indicate that up to that date, that is Nov. 8, 1749 at least, Washington had "layne" but a "few nights" in **Fredericktown.**

Now it is a well accepted local allegation that during the time when Washington was surveying in "Old Frederick" for Lord Fairfax, he occupied the little building at the northeast corner of Braddock and Cork Streets, called in recent years "Washington's Office", more frequently in the past "Washington's Headquarters". It is further alleged that he shared this office with George Johnston, a lawyer, that there he came to do the clerical work from time to time in connection with his surveying from 1749 to 1752.

When the ordinance providing for the purchase of this house was under consideration by the City Council on February 4, 1908, the question of the authenticity of the claim that this building had served as an office for George Washington when he was surveying for Lord Fairfax during the years 1749 to 1752 was raised, but the Council after discussion approved the purchase by a vote of 11 to 1. Before signing the ordinance, however, Mayor H. H. Baker made a detailed and careful study of this question, and in his report to the Council on March 3, 1908 concluded: "After a careful study of many records and the oral testimony of many reputable people, I believe that there is no reasonable doubt that the middle room was a block house and was used by Washington in tabulating his work as a surveyor when he was employed by Lord Fairfax." (*Winchester Council Journal* 1899-1909 - Page 393) The reader may see a more detailed report of this matter in Russell's *What I Know About Winchester* - Pages 42, 43, and 44.

In Mayor Baker's report to the Council he relies almost exclusively upon the research of Thomas K. Cartmell, Clerk of the Court of Frederick County, who was at that time (1908) working on his history of the County which was to be published the same year. In his book, when it did appear, Cartmell had the following to say about the building we are discussing:

"George Washington executed several deeds for tracts of land; the originals are on file in this office; he also purchased several tracts during the time he made the surveys

7

for Fairfax. One was from George Johnston, a member of the Winchester bar. The agreement for this purchase was executed in Winchester, and in the law office of Mr. Johnston. This office was used by Washington while in the town, when plotting his surveys. This office was located on the corner of Braddock Road and Cork Street; and tradition fixes the old stone and log building at that corner as 'Washington's Headquarters'. Whether this meant his military or surveyor's office is not known." (*Cartmell* - Page 250)

Washington made this purchase, which was for 552 acres on Bullskin Creek, on March 16, 1752 (*Freeman* Vol. One - Page 260), which was during his last surveying trip to the Valley.

The quotation from Cartmell above appears to us to be ambiguous and unconvincing. He says in the first place that the agreement by Washington to purchase the Johnston land "was executed in Winchester and in the law office of Mr. Johnston." We have been unable, after a careful search in the Frederick County records, to document this statement or to discover this agreement; but we shall accept it on the word of Mr. Cartmell, who was the Clerk of the Court and who allegedly saw this agreement. He next states categorically (without documentation) that the law office of Johnston was located in the building at the corner of Braddock and Cork Streets. A few sentences further on he says that the fact that Washington used this building as a "surveyor's office is not known".

We can see a number of logical objections to the allegation that Washington used this building as a sort of surveyor's office during the period from November, 1749 to May, 1752. First, there is his statement in the letter to "Richard" which we have quoted stating that he was in Frederick Town only a few nights during the 1749 surveying period. The record of his surveys from 1749 to 1752 shows that these surveys were located in the main far from Winchester, and that the image which Cartmell's statement calls up of a surveyor who went out and surveyed during the day and in the evening returned to the "office" on Cork Street to record his notes is a questionable if not false image. In fact, by the time Washington began his surveys, practically all of the lands in present-day Frederick County close to Winchester had already been surveyed, some as early as 1732. (*Friend's History* - Page 37)

8

In addition there is no evidence that George Johnston ever owned or leased the lot at the corner of Braddock and Cork Streets, and it seems to us to be rather far from the Court House to have served as a law office.

The other basis for Mayor Baker's approval of the purchase of the lot by the City was the traditions of the Kurtz family. These traditions according to Mr. Baker allege that Johann Adam Kurtz came to Winchester in 1749 and resided here during the years when Washington was surveying, that he passed on to his descendants the story that Washington used the house, which later became the Kurtz home, as a surveyor's office.

We can find no record of Johann Adam Kurtz, or for that matter any member of the Kurtz family, in either the deed books, Will books, or marriage register of Frederick County prior to 1778, when Adam Kurtz purchased the house we are considering. In Order Book No. 7 - Page 119 there is the record that at a Court held September 7, 1756 it was ordered that Adam Curtz be added to the list of titleables. The Adam Curtz named here appears undoubtedly to be the Adam Kurtz whom we are discussing; and the language of the record implies at least that he was a new arrival in the County.

It seems to us that to clarify somewhat the question we have been considering, we must detail the history of the land on which the alleged "Washington's Office" stands. It was in the proprietary of Thomas Lord Fairfax, but, either in ignorance of this fact or in defiance of it, the Governor and Council of Virginia about 1735 granted it to James Wood. We have been unable to find a record of this grant, but it is unquestionable that James Wood, certainly by 1744, thought that he had a clear title to it. When Fairfax denied the authority of the Governor and Council to make the grants of land in his proprietary, James Wood applied to the proprietor and in 1753 received a patent for his land. In 1752 he and Fairfax, with the approval of the House of Burgesses, laid out the Town of Winchester; and in 1758 Wood laid off the Wood's Addition to the Town of Winchester, again with the approval of the Burgesses. The house we are considering in this investigation stands on Lot Number 12 in Wood's Addition at the northeast corner of Braddock and

Cork Streets fronting 105 feet, 2 inches on Braddock Street and extending eastward on Cork Street 188 feet, 6 inches.

On September 5, 1759 Lot Number 12 in Wood's Addition was conveyed by James Wood to Thomas Rutherford for the sum of 20 pounds (*F.D.B.* 5 - Page 263). In a later conveyance, February 6, 1764, from Mary Wood widow of James Wood, to Thomas Rutherford of additional land on the east side of Braddock Street south of Lot Number 12, the property is described as "beginning about 60 feet from the corner of Lot 12 on the east side of Braddock Street on which Thomas Rutherford now lives" (*F.D.B.* 9 - Page 100). This record indicates that in 1764 Thomas Rutherford not only owned but lived on Lot Number 12, or, in other words, that there was a house on the lot at that date. On May 7, 1778 Thomas Rutherford sold to Adam Kurtz for 100 pounds the house and lot we are considering. (*F.D.B.* 17- Page 464)

The price of this lot, namely 100 pounds, as compared with the 20 pound purchase price further indicates that between 1759 and 1778 a house was built on the lot. The property remained in the possession of the Kurtz family until it was purchased by the City of Winchester on February 10, 1908. (*W.D.B.* 27 - Page 272)

It must be remembered, however, that during the period of Washington's surveys namely from 1749 to 1752, the land on which the alleged "Washington's Office" stands was held by James Wood under a tenuous and questionable title, and we have no evidence that he had built a house on it or good reason to conclude that he had.

We would conclude, then, from this rather tedious recital of facts and conjectures that we can not support the allegation that Washington used the building at the corner of Braddock and Cork Streets as a surveyor's office. Our belief is, supported by the diary of 1748 and other evidence, that when he came to old Frederick County to make a survey, he called first at Lord Fairfax's seat at *Greenway Court* and got his orders from the Proprietor, that he then departed for the area of the surveys, and that on their completion he returned to *Greenway Court* and there made whatever calculations and drawings were necessary to turn over to his Lordship for the issuance of patents. In this connection Mr. Stewart

Brown in his work *Virginia Baron, the Story of Thomas 6th Lord Fairfax* (Page 120) says:

> "The powerful, personable Washington spent several years working out of and at Greenway Court. Being an "omniverous reader", he enjoyed unrestricted access to the Proprietor's quite respectable library." (*Washington the Man and the Mason* Callahan - 38)

Before we conclude this discussion of "Washington's Office" we should ask and, if possible, answer the question: do the same objections which have been raised to the "Washington's Office" claim, apply also to the "Washington's Headquarters" claim? We hasten to reply in the negative to this question. On the contrary, there are many facts to make credible the claim that Washington used this building as headquarters when as Colonel of the Virginia Militia from the fall of 1755 until he moved into quarters at Fort Loudoun in Dec., 1756, he was charged by the Virginia Colony with the protection of its borders from the French and Indians. It is quite true that the problem concerning the erection of a building on what became Lot 12 remains, but 1755 was a time of War; James Wood was a loyal servant of the king; and there is every reason to believe that the part of the building which Mayor Baker appropriately called "the blockhouse" may have been built for military use. Its location is geographically ideal if we consider the following provable facts: (1) There was a war prisoners' stockade called "Fort George" on the hill back of the Braddock Street Church; (2) the drill ground was on the level area north of the headquarters; (3) Col. Washington lived in quarters on the site of the Kurtz building which he rented from William Cock; (4) the military hospital was on Loudoun Street south of the Kurtz house.

As will appear later in this study, the Journal of the Virginia House of Burgesses contains numerous claims from citizens for damages done or property seized during the period of 1755 to 1758 by the military under the command of Col. Washington.

On July 20, 1751 Robert Dinwiddie was appointed Governor of the Virginia Colony. Dinwiddie was a 58 year old Scot who had served a long and distinguished career as an official in Customs service of the British government. He was a stubborn and incor-

11

ruptible public servant, and in the years from 1753 to 1757 he and George Washington were to engage in a voluminous and sometimes stormy correspondence as each tried in his own way to do his duty. We shall discuss this later.

Dinwiddie discovered from the reports of traders and trappers before he had been in office a year that the French had moved into territory in the Ohio River Valley to which the British had a prior claim. By the fall of 1753 the situation had become intolerable, and it was feared that the French were preparing to build a fort at the forks of the Monongahela and Allegheny Rivers, headwaters of the Ohio. It was a vitally strategic location. Even as early as 1752 Dinwiddie had asked the Lords of Trade for money with which to build forts on the Ohio, particularly at the Forks. Upon the advice of his government in October of 1753 he decided to dispatch to the French Commanding Officer at Fort Le Boeuf on Lake Erie a message warning them of their encroachments and calling upon them to leave British territory. George Washington was thoroughly acquainted with the British land claims in the Ohio Valley. His brother Lawrence was one of the founders of the Ohio Company organized to acquire land and promote trade in that area. Lawrence died on July 26, 1752, and George inherited from his brother substantial land grants on the Ohio. He, therefore, had a personal interest in the alleged trespasses of the French, and promptly volunteered to be the bearer of Governor Dinwiddie's warning to the French. He was undoubtedly highly recommended for the responsibility by his good friend, William Fairfax. His offer was accepted at once.

He left Williamsburg on October 31, 1753 and in his report of his journey says:

"The next (day) I arrived at Fredericksburg, and engaged Mr. Jacob Vanbraam to be my French interpreter; and proceeded with him to Alexandria, where we provided Necessaries. From thence we went to Winchester, and got baggage, horses &c; and from thence we pursued the new Road to Wills Creek, where we arrived the 14th of November." (*Diaries* Vol. I - Page 43)

The "new road" mentioned here from Winchester to Wills Creek (Present day Cumberland, Maryland) seems to have followed roughly what was later to be called the Braddock Road, that is by present land-marks as follows: Route 522 - Whitacre - the Bloomery Gap - Little Cacapon Valley - crossing the Potomac at the Mouth of the Little Cacapon - Old Town, Maryland (then Cresaps) and Cumberland. (*Freeman* - Vol. I - Page 278 - Note 22)

We shall not here describe Washington's perilous journey to the French fort, other than to note that he uncovered clear evidence that they were planning a fort at the forks of the Ohio and that the reply to Dinwiddie warning was a brazen denial of his claims and an assertion that they proposed to continue their activities. If Washington stopped at Winchester on his return journey, he does not mention it in his report.

The French reply alarmed Governor Dinwiddie and he at once took steps to oppose them by military means. As a part of this military effort, on March 31, 1754 the Governor conferred on Washington the commission of Lieutenant-Colonel in the Virginia Regiment "with orders to take the troops, which were at that time quartered at Alexandria under my command, and to march with them towards the Ohio, there to aid Captain Trent in building Forts; and in defending the possessions of his Majesty against the attempts and hostilities of the French." (*Diaries* I - Page 73)

Washington's unit was to be part of a larger force to be commanded by Colonel Joshua Fry. Fry was born in Somersetshire, England and educated at Oxford. At one time he was professor of Mathematics at William and Mary College. He was a member of the Virginia House of Burgesses, participated in running a part of the boundary line between Virginia and North Carolina, and assisted Peter Jefferson with his well-known map of Virginia. Unfortunately on his way to Wills Creek his horse stumbled and fell and he was fatally injured, dying on May 31, 1754. His death left Lt. Col. Washington in full command of the expedition.

Washington left Alexandria on April 2, 1754 in command of 120 militiamen. (*Diaries* I - Page 74) He arrived at Winchester by way of Vestal's Gap on April 10, (*Freeman* - Page 345 - Note 126), and found there a company raised in Frederick County by Capt. Adam Stephen, which increased his total troop strength to 159 men. After impressing wagons and collecting other supplies, he departed from Winchester on April 18. (*Freeman* I - Page 348) He was vastly dissatisfied with the inefficiency of the preparations

13

at Winchester and with the cooperation of the local citizens which dissatisfaction he expressed to Governor Dinwiddie in a letter dated April 25, 1754 which read in part as follows:

"Out of seventy-four wagons impressed at Winchester, we got but ten after waiting a week; and some of those so badly, provided with teams that the soldiers were obliged to assist them up the hills, although it was known they had better teams at home. I doubt not that in some points I may have strained the law; but I hope, as my sole motive was to expedite the march, I shall be supported in it, should my authority be questioned, which at present I do not apprehend, unless some busybody intermeddles." (*Writings* - Vol. I - Page 41)

Washington's route from Winchester to Wills Creek appears to have been by what later became known as the Wappacomo or Romney Road. It left Winchester by present-day Fairmont Avenue, turned west into present-day Strother's Lane, thence by Stines Chapel, Albin, the Indian Hollow Road, Hayfield, Edward's Fort (present-day Capon Bridge), Pearsal's (present-day Romney), to Wills Creek (present-day Cumberland). (*Diaries* - I - Note 5, Page 73)

We shall not attempt here to describe the details of this expedition. As we have already indicated, Col. Fry, the commander of it, was killed, and Washington was left in full command. He was not properly supported by the Burgesses in Williamsburg, and after some initial success, was forced to surrender to the French at his improvised Fort Necessity on July 3, 1754. After a stop at

Wills Creek he hurried to Winchester and after a brief stay, on to Williamsburg. In November of 1754 he resigned as an officer in the Virginia regiment. Although he had been thanked by the House of Burgesses for his services in the late campaign against

the French, there can be little doubt that he felt that he had not been properly supported in that action, and he apparently mistrusted the home government in its dealings with militia officers as compared with British regulars.

Governor Dinwiddie was now thoroughly alarmed at the situation on the Ohio, and appealed to the home government for immediate and direct military help, that is British regulars. This time his appeal was heeded and an expedition consisting of two regiments of regular troops was dispatched to Virginia under the command of General Edward Braddock. The regiments were known as the "Irish Regiments" and consisted of the 44th Regiment, commanded by Sir Peter Halkett, and the 48th Regiment, commanded by Colonel Thomas Dunbar. The two regiments traveled by separate routes into old Frederick County. Sir Peter Halkett's 44th regiment marched from Alexandria, where the troops disembarked, through Virginia (part of the route being in present-day West Virginia) roughly by the following route: from Alexandria westward by the Braddock Road to its present terminus; from thence by an unknown road to "the Old Court House" near Tyson's Corner; thence to "Coleman's on Sugarland Run"; thence following roughly present-day Route 7 to its junction with present-day Route 9 at Clark's Gap; thence by Route 9 over the Blue Ridge at Vestals Gap and to present-day Charles Town; thence through Middleway crossing the Opequon near Brucetown and on by present-day Clearbrook and Hopewell Meeting House to the Widow Ballinger's on Apple Pie Ridge, now the home of William N. Hewitt; thence westward by present-day Lake St. Clair, Route 522, Whitacre, the Bloomery Gap to the Little Cacapon River Valley; down this to where it empties into the Potomac, thence crossing the Potomac and proceeding by Cresap's Plantation (present-day Oldtown, Maryland)) to Wills Creek (now Cumberland, Maryland.)

Colonel Dunbar's regiment, the 48th, crossed into Maryland at Rock Creek and proceeded to Frederick; thence over the South Mountain to Conococheque (present-day Williamsport); crossing here back into Virginia and going by Fort Evans joined the route of the 44th Regiment approximately at Clearbrook for the journey to Wills Creek. General Braddock accompanied this Regiment.

15

When he resigned from the militia in November of 1754, George Washington in a letter to Colonel William Fitzhugh said that he quit the service with reluctance and that "My inclinations are strongly bent to arms." (*Writings* Vol. I - Page 104-7) IIe was, therefore, stirred and tempted by the preparations in Williamsburg for the Braddock Expedition, and particularly by the fact that Virginia and other colonial troops were to be included in the effort. He soon wrote a letter of congratulations to General Braddock on his arrival in America, which apparently made it clear to the General that young Washington might be available for service in the campaign. At any rate on March 2, 1755 Robert Orme, the General's Aid de Camp wrote to Washington saying that the General "will be very glad of your company in his family." (*Hamilton* I - Pages 57-58). The invitation was quickly accepted, with the understanding that Washington was to serve without pay and was to be allowed to terminate his service as an Aide to the General upon the completion of the campaign.

Braddock planned a conference with Benjamin Franklin and Governor Sharpe of Maryland at Frederick, Maryland on his way to Wills Creek; and in anticipation of meeting the General there when the conference took place, Washington left Mount Vernon on April 23, 1755 with four horses, little money, light baggage and a single pair of boots; (*Writings* - I - Pages 116-117-119) and journeyed to his Bullskin property in the Shenandoah Valley. Here he remained until April 30, when he crossed the Potomac at Swearingen's Ferry, Shepherdstown, and rode over the South Mountain to Frederick. (*Account Book to Thomas Swearingen* 4 shillings 9 pence). On May 2 along with Governor Sharpe and General Braddock he rode back to Swearingen's Ferry. (*Sharpe* I - Pages 205-208). Here Governor Sharpe left the party and returned to Annapolis, but before so doing presented his chariot to the General, which Braddock accepted on condition that he be permitted to purchase the outfit. This decision was based on the fact that Braddock's coach was too large and too heavy for the makeshift roads of Virginia and Maryland. (*Sharpe* I - 205-208)

The General then rode with Washington, after crossing the Potomac to Shepherdstown, to Winchester, arriving there on May 3. Washington and Braddock while they were in Winchester on this occasion stopped at the inn of William Cock, which stood on the site of the Kurtz house at 21 South Loudoun Street. (*Quarles* - Old Homes - Page 182). An entry of May 6, 1755 in Washington's Account Book - Ledger A, Folio 21 records that Washington paid to "a servant maid at Mr. Cock's" five shillings. Braddock came to Winchester with Washington because he had been led to believe by Governor Dinwiddie that Indian Chiefs would meet him there who could be persuaded to join in the campaign against the French. No such Indians appeared at Winchester and the General was further irritated at what he regarded as colonial inefficiency.

Washington used the stop at Winchester to apply for and receive a loan of 40 pounds from Lord Fairfax with which to replace three of the four horses he had started out with. (*Writings* I -Page 119) On May 7, 1755 he left with Braddock to join the troops on their way to Wills Creek. (*Freeman* II - Page 33)

On May 15, 1755 Braddock dispatched Washington to Hampton to receive 4000 pounds which was required for meeting the expenses of the expedition and on May 16 he passed through Winchester on this journey. (*Writings* I - Page 128) He returned to Winchester on May 27, but was required to wait until a cavalry escort came to escort him with the money to the Army, now well beyond Wills Creek. He complained bitterly of this delay in a letter to John Augustine Washington in a not-too-complimentary reference to Winchester: "I shou'd have received greater relief from the fatigues of my journey, and my time wou'd have been spent much more agreeably, had I halted below (*that is below the Blue Ridge*), rather than at this vile post but I little imagin'd I shou'd have occasion to wait for a guard who ought to have waited for me." (*Writings* I - 129-30) Finally after waiting two days he "made use of a small Guard of the Militia of Frederick" County and went on with his precious cargo. (*Writings* I - 133)

It will not be our purpose here to describe further the details of the Braddock expedition to Fort Duquesne or of his tragic defeat there. Let it suffice to say that in the engagement there, Washington conducted himself with great distinction and bravery which earned him the respect and plaudits of the British staff. He seems to have been received with trust and real affection by the ill-starred General, and well founded tradition has it that he read the burial service at his funeral. By July 24 he was back in Winchester on his way home, arriving at Mount Vernon on July 26. (*Writings* I - 153)

The defeat of Braddock and the deaths of both the General and Sir Peter Halkett left Col. Thomas Dunbar in command of the British force. After much confusion of counsel and despite the bitter opposition of Governor Dinwiddie, Dunbar withdrew to Philadelphia, and the Virginia frontier was left to the mercy of the French and Indians. The immediate responsibility for meeting this challenge devolved upon the Governor and the House of Burgesses. Both of these were much impressed with the reports of Washington's behavior at Fort Duquesne. Accordingly on August 14, 1755 Governor Dinwiddie appointed Washington "Colonel of the Virginia Regiment and Command-in-Chief of all the Forces now raised and to be raised for the Defense of His Majesty's Colony and for repelling the unjust and hostile Invasions of the French and their Indian Allies." (*Dinwiddie* II - 184) The Governor further directed that "As Winchester is the highest place of rendezvous which is exposed to the enemy, you are hereby required to make it your headquarters." (*Ibid* - 185)

After a month of preparation in Alexandria and Fredericksburg Washington, now a full Colonel and Commander-in-Chief, set out for Winchester, arriving on September 14. Here he issued a number of orders and may be said to have formally established his headquarters. From this time until December of 1758 he was to spend a major part of his time in Winchester. It is true that there were occasions when he was away for rather lengthy periods: for example from February 4, 1756 to April 7, 1756, when he rode to Boston to confer with Governor William Shirley; and from November 10, 1757 to April 4, 1758 when he was seriously ill at Mount Vernon; but in the main Winchester was his base of operations.

In March of 1756 the Virginia House of Burgesses upon the recommendation of Governor Dinwiddie passed an act indicating what the defense of the western frontier of the Colony would be. This act provided "that a chain of forts shall be erected, to begin at Henry Enochs, on Great-Cape-Capon, in the County of Hampshire, and to extend to the South Fork of Mayo-River, in the County of Halifax, to consist of such a number and at such distance from each other, as shall be thought necessary and directed by the Governor, or Commander-in-Chief of this Colony." (*Hening* - Vol. VII - P. 17-18) It is assumed that Washington as Commander-in-Chief agreed with this as a temporary strategy, but there is much in his correspondence to show that he preferred an offensive approach and that he believed that the French and Indian threat would be removed only by destroying its source.

The "forts" mentioned in this act of the Assembly appear to have been of three kinds: block-houses, stockades, and forts. Louis K. Koontz in his valuable work, *The Virginia Frontier*, 1754 - 1763 - Page 99 et seq., has this to say of these structures:

> "The block - houses were simple, two storied, log buildings, and square, having the second story project beyond the lower .... The stockade — a kind of fort with palisade — much stronger than the block - house. It was usually a double log structure, two stories in height, surrounded at a distance by a high fence of stakes driven into the ground. The forts were the most pretentious of the fortifications, combining as a rule the features of both the other kinds of buildings. They were generally rectangular, having blockhouses at the four corners and these connected by a palisaded fence.
>
> The stockades and forts were more than posts for garrisons; they were the places of refuge to which the people in the vicinity flocked, and in which they sought shelter when Indians made attacks in the neighborhood."

Dr. Koontz was able to identify and describe 81 of these forts on the Virginia frontier. We are convinced that there was a fourth kind of structure to which the frontier settlers applied the name "fort", and that was a substantial dwelling or outbuilding usually of stone, to which drinking water was accessible either from a spring in the cellar or piped into the house from a nearby source, into which loop-holes for firing had been designed. We can name a number of such so-called forts in Old Frederick County which do not appear on the Koontz list: such as, Fort Bowman, Fort Fry, Fort White, Fort George in Winchester, Fort Helm and others.

Among other measures which the Governor and the Burgesses adopted for the defense of the frontier was the appropriation of 40,000 pounds to augment the Virginia forces to 2000 men. (*Din-*

widdie II - Pages 96-145) Later squads of Rangers (mounted militia) to patrol the areas between forts and provide punitive expeditions against Indian marauders were organized. We should be careful here to distinguish between the enlisted militia or volunteers who signed up for specific terms in the service and the County Militia who in emergencies were drafted into service for the time of the emergency. The 2000 man militia force which was authorized by the Burgesses (never, however, fully realized) was of the former of these groups.

With the major responsibility for implementing these and other measures Colonel George Washington, twenty-three years old, went to work on September 14, 1755 in Winchester.

There has been a tendency among some historians to treat the Virginia border war of 1755 to 1758 as a sort of comic opera conflict; and indeed there were many ludicrous aspects of it. However, the evidence is plain that though limited in scope, it was a bitter and bloody conflict. In a letter to Lord Loudoun in January 1757 Washington wrote:

> "For in the course of this campaign, since March I mean (as we have had but one constant campaign and continued scene of action, since we first entered the service) our troop has been engaged in upwards of twenty skirmishes, and we have had near an hundred men killed and wounded, from a small regiment dispersed over the country, and acting upon the defensive, as ours is by order." (*Writings* 2 - Page 11)

In October of the same year in a letter to Col. John Stanwix he wrote:

> "We have had several visitations from the enemy, and much mischief done, since my last to you. About the 17th ultimo there were upwards of twenty persons killed only twelve miles from this garrison, and notwithstanding I sent a strong detachment from here (Winchester) to pursue them, and ordered the passes of the mountains to be waylaid by commands from other places, yet we were not able to meet with these savages." (*Writings* - 2 - Page 144)

In the same month and year in a letter from Winchester to John Robinson, Speaker of the House of Burgesses, he wrote:

"It will be necessary to observe to you that the inhabitants of this fertile and (once) populous valley, are now become our most western settlers, save the few families that are forted on the Branch; that the enemy have, in great measure, ceased committing hostilities on the Branch, and fallen upon the people of this valley; and that a considerable part of them have already removed." (*Writings* - 2 - 52)

A letter of William Fairfax to Washington on May 9, 1756 recites that Col. James Wood, the founder of Winchester and Clerk of the Frederick County Court because of the atrocities of the French and Indians had removed "with his family" from his plantation at Winchester and that this had "added to the fears of many people below, thinking he would not desert his plantation without the utmost necessity". (*Hamilton* I - Page 252)

Washington's most difficult problem was the recruiting of men and officers to man the forts along the frontier, and the maintenance of discipline among these officers and men. In a letter to Col. Henry Lee on July 1, 1757 he laid down the rather unique physical requirements for recruits for the Regiment:

"You are to proceed to Fredericksburg, where you are to remain for the reception of the Draughts for the Regiment. You are to take their names, size, complexion, age, country, and former employment; and the officer's names who deliver them: specifying the number you receive from each officer; to whom you are to give a receipt for them. You must not receive any that are subject to fits, or that have ulcers or old sores on their legs, or any other disease that renders them incapable of service; nor that are under five feet four inches high, unless active and well built." (*Writings* 2 - Page 83)

On July 29, 1757 Washington issued Instructions to the Captains of Companies. This is a lengthy and altogether remarkable document, a strong tribute to the maturity and judgement of the young Commander-in-Chief. (*Writings* 2 - Pages 109-114) His various orders display his intense desire to instill discipline and to make particularly the garrison at Winchester a respectable military establishment. Following are some of the orders to support this statement:

Orders, Winchester May 1, 1756
"Any soldier, who shall presume to quarrel or fight shall receive five hundred lashes, without benefit of Court

Martial. Any soldier found drunk shall immediately receive one hundred lashes, without benefit of Court Martial." (*Writings* - I - Page 353)

Orders July 22, 1756

"The Adjutant must acquaint all the town's people that they must not allow soldiers to be drunk in their Houses, or sell them any liquors, without an order from a Commissioned Officer; or else they may depend Colonel Washington will prosecute them as the Act of Assembly directs. This precaution must be particularly given to the Dutch Baker, John Stewart, and Jacob Sowers." (*Writings* I - Page 409)

"Soldiers - - in case of an alarm must repair to the Court House, and draw up under the hill before the Court House Door, being the usual alarm post." (*Ibid*)

Orders September 25, 1756

"The men are to parade at beating the long roll tomorrow morning at 10 o'clock; to be marched as usual to the Fort, to attend Divine Services. The Officers to be present at calling the roll, and see that the men do appear in the most decent manner they can." (*Writings* - I -Page 473)

Orders - November 9, 1756

"Tomorrow being the aniversary of His Majesty's Birthday, the men to be drawn up at 12 o'clock, and marched to the Fort, there to fire three volleys, which is to be taken from the cannon: Officers to appear in their Regimentals; and the soldiers to dress as clean as possible." (*Writings* - I - Page 507)

Orders - Winchester August 7, 1756

"As every method hitherto practiced has been found ineffectual to restrain the paltry tippling house ai. : gin shops in this town from selling liquor, contrary to orders, to the soldiers, to the detriment of His Majesty's Service, and irreparable loss of their own health. It is hereby expressly ordered, that as many men as the tents will contain do immediately encamp; and all the rest, except those in the hospital, be on Monday new quartered upon Brinker, Heath, and Lemon; who are charged not to sell more than a reasonable quantity of liquor, and at reasonable rates to each man per day; as they will answer the contrary. And any soldier or Draught who is found drinking in any of the other houses, or who is known to purchase, by direct or indirect means, any liquor from other places; or who shall be found going into, or sitting down in any of the other houses, without giving a sufficient excuse why he did so, shall immediately receive 50 lashes without the benefit of a Court Martial." (*Writings* - 2 - Page 440)

There can be little doubt that Washington exercised strong methods to insure that proper discipline was maintained. One of the major problems was desertion. In a letter from Winchester to John Stanwix on July 15, 1757 he describes what he proposes to do to cure this problem:

"I have a gallows near 40 feet high erected (which has terrified the rest exceedingly), and I am determined if I can be justified in the proceeding, to hang two or three on it, as an example to others." (*Writings* - 2 - Page 97)

Just a short time after the foregoing, or on August 3, 1757, in a letter to Governor Dinwiddie, he discloses the fact that what he planned to do had been done:

"I send your Honour a copy of the proceedings of a General Court Martial. Two of those condemned, namely Ignatius Edwards and William Smith, were hanged on Thursday just before the companies marched to their respective posts. Your Honor will, I hope, excuse my hanging stead of shooting them. It conveyed much more terror to other; and it was for example sake we did it. They were proper objects to suffer: Edwards had deserted twice before, and Smith was accounted one of the greatest villains upon the continent. Those who were intended to be whipped, have received their punishments accordingly." (*Writings* II - Page 118)

The young Commander-in-Chief did not limit his punishments to privates, but did not hesitate to take to task even the wife of one of his officers when the occasion demanded. In a letter to Capt. John Ashby on December 28, 1755, he says:

"There are continual complaints to me of the misbehavior of your wife; who, I am told, sows sedition among the men, and is chief of every mutiny. If she is not immediately sent from the camp, or I hear any more complaints of such irregular behavior, upon my arrival there; I shall take care to drive her out myself, and suspend you." (*Writings* - I - Page 264)

That Washington had a low opinion of the militia is attested to by many of his letters. When we use the term "Militia" here, and when he used it, we are referring not to the men who enlisted for a stated term, but rather to the County Militia. In the rather frequent alarms concerning anticipated Indian attacks, militia companies from the Counties east of the Blue Ridge would be rushed to Winchester, many of them utterly untrained and in many cases without weapons. Large numbers would desert on the way; and when they arrived in Winchester would become eager patrons of the "Tippling House Keepers". In a letter to Col. John Stanwix from Fort Loudoun on July 15, 1757, Washington voiced his complete lack of confidence in these warriors:

> "Militia, you will find, Sir, will never answer your expectation, no dependence is to be placed upon them; they are obstinate and perverse, thy are often egged on by the officers, who lead them to acts of disobedience, and when they are ordered to certain posts for the security of stores, or the protection of the inhabitants, will, on a sudden, resolve to leave them . . . . no man I can conceive was ever worse plagued than I have been with the Draughts that were sent from the several counties in this Government, to complete its regiment; out of 400 that were received at Fredericksburg and at this place, 114 have deserted."
> (*Writings* 2 - Page 97)

One of the major responsibilities which Washington had in Winchester was that of overseeing the planning and building of Fort Loudoun. The Fort was authorized by an Act of the Virginia House of Burgesses, March 17, 1756. (*Hening* - Vol. 7 - Page 34). In a letter to Governor Dinwiddie from Winchester, dated May 23, 1756, Washington wrote:

> "At this place I have begun the Fort according to your orders." (*Writings* - I - Page 388)

Prior to that date in a letter to Col. Adam Stephen from Winchester on May 18, 1756 he wrote:

> "I am here detained to construct and erect a fort, which the Governor has ordered to be done with expedition. As it will be necessary to have a number of carpenters etc. to carry on the work with spirit and vigor; you are desired to send down all the men of Captain George Mercer's company; those that are there of Captain Bell's; all the men that are skilled in masonry: and if all these do not make up fifty; you are to complete the party to that

number, out of the best carpenters in other companies."
(*Writings* - I - Page 379)

Note: Col. Stephen and the troops mentioned were at this date stationed at Fort Cumberland.

Other references to the progress of the work on the Fort occur frequently in the correspondence and orders of Colonel Washington in the period from 1756 to 1758. Washington drew the plan for the Fort, the original of which is to be found in the Library of Congress. It is certain that he obtained help in the plan from William Fairfax of Belvoir as the following quotation from a letter of Fairfax to Washington on July 10, 1756 will confirm:

> "I received yours of the 22nd ult. by Jenkins—enclosing two plans of the intended Fort you are erecting at Winchester, but the bastions of the different plans appearing to vary in the dimensions. You have not distinguished which is the one made use of; however, as I apprehend your scale is feet. I think either of them well designed and notwithstanding Col. Innes invidious calling it a Citadel will be as small as can be formed to receive and entertain a suitable garrison for that part of the country and expected to sustain the lesser fortresses on the frontier. You having represented on that side of the Fort marked O there is an hill at about 100 yards distance which forms and overlooks a second valley so as to cover an Enemy's approach where also the most likely to begin an attack, I think it advisable to build a redoubt on that hill as soon as the greater works begin to be defensible. And as the practice of sallying out is to interrupt and destroy the first breaking of ground and near approaches of the enemy whilst entrenching and raising of batteries, I have marked the Sally Port on the same curtain. In the passage through the wall, which should be kept clear during war or apprehended invasion, there should be two strong doors, especially the outermost, well studded with large nails, substantial locks and Barrs for the further security thereof against the enemy's shot and fire, a blind like a Ravelin necessary to conceal the Sally Port. It is many years since I was in one, but if I mistake not, they are so guarded." (*Hamilton* - Vol. I - Page 310)

Other references in Washington's writing and in letters to him concerning progress on Fort Loudoun follow:

> "*Winchester July* 30, 1756 — *Order to the Inhabitants of Winchester*
>
> Colonel Washington takes this method to inform the in-

habitants of this Town that the militia will be discharged in a short time and consequently the completing of the Fort will be much retarded. He, therefore, hopes and desires that every family in Town will send a man to work upon it; and that every young fellow, without the charge of a family, will readily give his assistance towards it." (*Writings* - I - Page 413)

"*January 12, 1757 — Letter to Gov. Dinwiddie from Fort Cumberland*

"When I left Winchester, I gave directions about carrying on the works at Fort Loudoun with all possible dispatch. But a letter from Captain Mercer - - - informs me that they are at a loss in respect to the manner of making the ambrasures thro the parapet; although I gave directions in person before I came away on this head; they propose a method that will spoil the whole work. And as I could not make them sensible of my plan by instruction only when present, I have little hope of accomplishing it by writing, consequently I am reduced to a disagreeable dilemma." (*Writings* - 2 - Page 2)

May 30 1757 — Letter to Gov. Dinwiddie from Fort Loudoun

"The works at Fort Loudoun go on slowly with the small number of men now employed, that I despair of getting tru in time." (*Writings* - 2 - Page 42)

June 25, 1757 — Letter to William Fairfax from Fort Loudoun

"Our soldiers labour on the public works with great spirit and constancy from Monday morning till Sunday night." (*Writings* - 2 - Page 75)

June 27, 1757 — Letter to Gov. Dinwiddie from Fort Loudoun

"We are indifatigably assiduous in forwarding the workmen; all work from daylight to daylight, Sundays not excepted, and but one hour in the day allowed for eating, etc. But it is impossible that so small a number of men as we have had and now have at work, can be imagined sufficient to complete such a vastly heavy piece of work in a much greater time than you mention. Nay, 300 men could hardly finish it by next October. And as with our present number it will require a considerable time to put it in a tolerable posture of defence; and as the great importance of this place renders the completion of its works so necessary; I hope you will give me leave to employ at least

Colonel James Wood of Winchester as proxy for George Washington, being chaired through the streets of Winchester on the occasion of Washington's election to the Virginia House of Burgesses from Frederick County July 24, 1758. This drawing appeared first in Graham's Magazine in 1853 according to Mrs. Greene's *Winchester Virginia and Its Beginnings*.

Appeal of the People of Winchester to Washington for Protection against the French and Indians.

From a drawing by Felix O. Darley which appeared first in Washington Irving's Life of Washington. A painting from this drawing appeared for many years on the ceiling of the old Empire Theater at the northwest corner of Rouss Avenue and Cameron Street. When this building was torn down, the Farmers and Merchants Bank, which had acquired the property, recovered the painting (which was on canvas), and its restored form may be seen in the bank today. Also in 1932 on the occasion of the celebration of the bicentennial of the birth of Washington, the Winchester-Frederick County Historical Society commissioned the Artist *Burtis Baker* to paint a copy of the Darley Drawing, which appears on the west wall of the Handley Library reading room today.

double its present garrison upon them when the Draughts come up." (*Writings* - 2 - Page 78)

August 3, 1757 — Letter to Gov. Dinwiddie from Fort Loudoun

"And there now remains here no more than Capt. Stewart's company and my own, except about 40 workmen, which I took from the Draughts to work at this place." (*Writings* - 2 - Page 118)

September 24, 1757 — Letter to Gov. Dinwiddie from Fort Loudoun

"I understand that there are a mortar and a number of shells for it at Williamsburg, which would be of infinite service here, tho little or none where they are. We have a quantity of round and grape shot for six pounders, but no cannon to use them. A few pieces of that size would be a great addition to our strength; and as this is the only place we have (were it finished) where a stand could be made, in case of any formidable attack, I can conceive nothing in our power should be omitted to make it as defensible as we can." (*Writings* - 2 - Page 136)

October 8, 1757 — Letter to Col. John Stanwix from Fort Loudoun

"These constant alarms and perpetual movements of the soldiers of this garrison have almost put a stop to the progress of the public works at this place." (*Writings* - 2 - Page 146)

February 23, 1758 — Letter from Captain Charles Smith from Fort Loudoun to Washington

"Concerning the works at Fort Loudoun has gone on tolerable well in your absence. The Third Barrack is entirely covered in and the last one now aframing in order to raise. The parapet on the last curtain is up, the last bastion is laid over with logs, and two of the Ambusiers done and now is about the other four: we have done all the Joyner's work in the Second Barrack. We are in great want of a barrel of double tens for the last Barrack, we not having one. Our Stonemasons have been sick ever since you went away . . . . The well has been almost full of water, but now is cleared and they are at work in it again, and is near ninety foot deep." (*Hamilton* II - Page 268)

May 4, 1758 — Letter to John Blair from Fort Loudoun

"If the works here are to be completed, which from their great importance I should think highly necessary, in that event, an additional number of 60 or 80, good men from the militia, for that particular service would be wanted." (*Writings* - 2 - Page 195)

May 2, 1758 — Letter to John Blair from Williamsburg
"I should be glad to know if the works at Fort Loudoun are still to go on? In what manner to be forwarded? And under whose direction? Nothing surely will contribute more to the public weal than the fort when completed." (*Writings* - 2 -- Page 205)

Fort Loudoun was built on Outlot Number 49, a five acre tract laid off by John Baylis at the behest of Lord Fairfax and James Wood when the Town of Winchester was chartered in 1752. This outlot, together with Inlot Number 32, was granted to Isaac Parkins at that time. (*Props. Grants* - Book M. Page 349) It is assumed that, when the outlot was needed as the site of a fort for the defense of the Colony, Parkins, who was a patriot, raised no objection, or, if he did, it was seized anyway as a military necessity. Other private property was seized at the same time, and when the crisis was over, local citizens whose property was seized petitioned the House of Burgesses for damages sustained. Many such petitions appear in the Journal of the House of Burgesses among them one of December 8, 1762 as follows:

"Petition of Robert Rutherford and Mary Wood in behalf of themselves and others, praying that they may be paid by the publick for timber taken off their respective lands and made use of in building Fort Loudoun in Winchester." (*Journal of House of B.* - 1761-65 - Page 139)

Washington himself prior to 1755 had acquired Inlot Number 77 and Outlot Number 16 in the Town of Winchester. (*Props. Grants* - Book H - Page 394) Inlot 77 had a frontage of 119 feet on Braddock Street and extended eastward on Fairfax Lane 188 feet, 6 inches. It joined Outlot 49 on which the Fort was built. Of this lot the Historian Kercheval has this to say:

"Our highly respected and venerable general, John Smith, who settled in Winchester in 1773, informed the author that he had seen and conversed with some of Washington's officers soon after he settled in Winchester, and they stated to him that Washington marked out the site of the Fort, and superintended the work; that he bought a lot in Winchester, erected a smith's shop on it, and brought from Mount Vernon his own blacksmith to make the necessary iron work for the fort." (*Kercheval* - Page 70)

Fort Loudoun was never fully completed, but by the fall of 1757 its essential parts were built, and it is said to have been reconnoitered by French officers and found impregnable. The fort covered half an acre and was a redoubt with four bastions. The well to supply the Fort with water was sunk 103 feet through solid limestone. It mounted fourteen cannon: 6 eighteen pounders; 6 twelve pounders; four swivel guns; two howitzers. All but one of these, a six pounder, were removed during the Revolution to be used elsewhere. William Greenway Russell in his *What I Know about Winchester* (Page 79) recalls how in 1824 a crowd of New Years day revelers went to the ruins of Fort Loudoun and with charges previously prepared fired several rounds from the old weapon, the concussion breaking twenty or more panes from old Mrs. Peyton's windows, whose home was nearby on North Loudoun Street. The culprits feared her wrath, but she forgave them in the spirit of the season.

The Rev. Andrew Barnaby, an English clergyman, who visited Winchester in the spring of 1760, has this to say of Fort Loudoun:

> "It is a regular square fortification, with four bastions, mounting twenty-four cannon; the length of each curtain, if I am not mistaken, is about eight yards. Within there are barracks for 450 men. The materials of which it is constructed are logs filled up with earth; the soldiers attempted to surround it with a dry ditch; but the rock was so extremely hard and inpenetrable, that they were obliged to desist. It is still unfinished, and, I fear, going to ruin; for the assembly (House of Burgesses), who seldom look a great way before them, after having spent about 9000 pounds currency on it, cannot be prevailed upon to give another thousand towards finishing it, because we are in possession of Pittsburg (Fort Duquesne); and as they suppose, quite secure on this account; yet it is certain, that, in case of another Indian War on this side, which is by no means improbable, considering our general treatment of that people, it would be of the utmost advantage and security." (*Barnaby* - Pages 51-64)

The Rev. Philip Vickers Fithian, itinerant Presbyterian preacher who spent a short time at Stephens City in 1775 and preached at the old Opequon Church at Kernstown a number of times, writing on May 22, 1775 said of Winchester: "North of the Town are the ruins of an old fort wasted and crumbled down by time!" (*Fithian* - Page 13)

Thomas Anburey a young British officer, who was captured at the surrender of General Burgoyne at Saratoga, and who in 1780 was a prisoner of war in Winchester, in a letter written November 20, 1780 seems to contradict Fithian's description of the ruined condition of the garrison when he says:

"The barracks are still remaining, which will contain with ease and comfort, near five hundred men, and upon emergency would contain twice as many, as is the case at present, there being near that number of our soldiers quartered in them." (*Anburey* - Letter LXXI)

Not the least of Washington's worries in Winchester during the French and Indian War was that of handling the allegedly "friendly" Indians. Dinwiddie and subsequent governors, observing the assistance afforded the French by their Indian allies, tried desperately to secure similar help from Indians who professed to side with the British, but without any appreciable success. It is clear to us that Washington did not share Dinwiddie's hopes for effecive Indian aid; that he rather regarded those who did come to Winchester presumably to help as something of a nuisance. To further exacerbate the situation the Governor insisted on having at the headquarters an Indian Agent responsible directly to him and not to the Commander-in-Chief.

Washington also had some difficulty apparently in reconciling the soldiers and townspeople to their Indian allies as indicated by the following order:

Orders — October 28, 1756

"As Colonel Washington is to hold conference with the Catawba Indians; betwixt eleven and twelve o'clock, he desires all the Officers in Town to attend at that time. And during the time of the conference, he orders a Sargeant and Drummer beat through the Town ordering all Soldiers and TownsPeople to use the Indians civilly and kindly; to avoid giving them liquor and to be cautious what they speak before them: as all of them understand English, and ought not to be affronted." (*Writings* - 1 - Page 486)

As the time drew near for the second attack on Fort Duquesne by General Forbes, the number of Indians passing through Winchester on their way to the scene of action increased. For example on April 9, 1758 in a letter from Winchester to John Blair, Washington says:

> "About 400 Indians have come to this place . . . and most of them are gone out to the War. One hundred and forty more are expected in today, and numerous other parties are upon their march to join us." (*Writings* - 2 - Page 172)

These Indians were Cherokees and Catawbas from the south who shortly after the date indicated in the above letter returned to their homes. From the time they entered the southern borders of the Colony of Virginia until they returned they were guilty of every sort of disorder and thievery. When the War was over the Burgesses were constantly besieged with petition from citizens requesting recompense for damages done by these Indian allies.

We are naturally interested in where Col. Washington lived in Winchester during the period from the fall of 1755 until the fall of 1758. Prior to December 2, 1756 of this period he headed his letters from this location Winchester, but on December 2 his letter to Gov. Dinwiddie is headed *Fort Loudoun*. We can, therefore, assume that from that date on quarters had been provided for him at the Fort. Tradition has it that the "room in the Fort used by Washington" was "above the gateway commanding a View of Main Street." (*Morton* - Page 74) An entry in Washington's Account Book dated December 4, 1756 records that on that date he paid 40 pounds to "Captain Cocks for rent of his house." (Ledger A.) This was evidently a yearly rental and indicates that prior to December 1756 he had lived in the Cock house. Where was this house? It was on Inlot Number 8 in the 1752 plan by John Baylis for the Town of Winchester. It fronted a distance of 119 feet on the west side of South Loudoun Street, extended westward 189 feet, 9 inches, and had an area of about one half acre. In terms of present day landmarks the frontage of Lot Number 8 on Loudoun Street extended from the Town Run to the south line of Patton's Furniture Company, and it ran westward to Indian Alley.

By a patent dated May 15, 1753 Lord Fairfax conveyed Lot Number 8 to William Cocks. (*Props. Grants* - Book H - Page 325) William Cocks' last name is spelled in the various documents of the time Cock, Cocks, Cocke, and Cox. Cocks was a Captain of Rangers in the French and Indian War, and there are many communications to him in the correspondence of Col. George Washington. Two letters, dated June 7 and 28, 1755 written by Washington to his brother John Augustine directed that mail to him should be sent "in care of Mr. Cock of Winchester." (*Writings* - I - Pages 139 and 145) He appears to have been a bachelor, and as an officer of the Rangers was away from Winchester a great deal. His house would have been available for rental to the Colonel in command of the Virginia forces on the frontier of the Colony. We have already recorded also the fact that Washington and General Braddock spent several days at the Cock Tavern in 1755.

In his will, probated November 7, 1769 William Cocks left his estate, including Lot 8 to John Lemley and to his "well-loved friend Robert Rutherford". (*F.W.B.* - 3 - Page 508) In the same year Lot 8 was purchased by James Gamul Dowdall, who built in 1792 the stone house which appears on the lot today at 21 South Loudoun Street. (*F.D.B.* 13 - Page 267) It was later to become the Kurtz house. (*W.D.B.* 22 - Page 95).

There is an entry in the Account Book of Colonel Washington for August 18, 1758 recording the payment "By my expenses at Mr. Hite's to ye date hereof as pr. account rendered 85 pounds 5. 4. 3/4." (*Ledger A*) It is obvious from the substantial amount of this payment that it perhaps represents payment for lodgings and entertainment from time to time. The "Mr. Hite" referred to must have been Yost Hite who conducted an inn at present-day Bartonsville, where Washington and the surveying party to which he belonged stopped briefly in 1748.

We may, we think, conclude that prior to December of 1756 when quarters were provided for him in Fort Loudoun, and from perhaps time to time after that, Washington slept at the Cocks house on South Loudoun Street in Winchester or at Yost Hite's Inn at Bartonsville.

Following are quoted records from sundry sources which will, we believe throw some light on the period when Colonel Washington commanded the colonial troops at Winchester on the colonial frontier and upon the places and people in Winchester:

October 18, 1755 — *Letter from Gov. Dinwiddie to Washington*

"I think there are near 500 beeves from N. Carolina near Winchester. Give directions about them." (*Hamilton* - I - Page 113)

October 20, 1755 — *Orders*

"To the Commanding Officer of the Troops which shall arrive here from Fredericksburg and Alexandria: The Court House Barracks at Lemons are allotted for your men." (*Writings* I - Page 219)

Note: "Lemons" was about where the Conrad House stood at 12 North Cameron Street. (*Props. Grants* - Book H - Page 356)

November 9, 1756 — *Letter of Washington to Speaker of House of Burgesses, John Robinson*

"A Chaplain for the Regiment ought to be provided; that we may at least have the show, if we are said to want the substance of Godliness." (*Writings* - I - Page 505)

May 11, 1756 — *Memoranda Respecting the Militia*

"Colo. Spottswood from Spottsylvania with 3 Field Officers, 5 Captains, 10 Subalterns, and 130 private men arrived here and encamped in Colo. Wood's Meadow." (*Writings* - I - Page 348)

September 23, 1756 — *Orders of Col. Washington*

"The Quartermaster is to provide a lock and key for the Town House, and secure all the windows above and below with hides." (*Writings* - I - Page 472)

Note: Concerning the location of the "Town House" we can only guess. Perhaps it was located where the Market House was to be, or perhaps it was the Market House, which stood where the City Hall stands today.

September 25, 1756 — *Orders of Col. Washington*

"The men are to parade at beating the long roll tomorrow morning at 10 o'clock; to be marched as usual to the Fort to attend Divine Service; the Officers to be present at calling the roll, and see that the men do appear in the most decent manner they can." (*Writings* - I - Page 473)

July 10, 1757 — *Letter of Col. Washington to Gov. Dinwiddie*

"Very few of the Draughts have arms; I have several smiths employed in repairing the old ones in store here, which can scarcely be made serviceable. They can be completed with Bayonets and cartouch (powder box) boxes. It was not until lately I have been able to procure an Armorer." (*Writings* 2 - Page 88)

July 12, 1757 — Letter of Col. Washington to Gov. Dinwiddie

"The Philadelphia post, which formerly came to this place, being stopped, prevents our hearing any foreign news: but what are transmitted in the channel of friendly letters. We greatly regret the loss of this post, and would gladly keep it up by private subscription, from this to Carlyle, if it comes (to) that length." (*Writings* 2 - Page 98)

Note: Post offices of the Colonies were at that time under the management of Benjamin Franklin and Col. John Hunter. The Assembly of Pennsylvania, when Braddock marched west, had established a special post from Winchester to Philadelphia "for the accommodation of the army chiefly."

July 24, 1757 — Letter of Col. Washington to Lieut. Thomas Bullitt

"It was a mistake in the Quarter-Master, that he did not send Hats for your Company, Garters, and Buckles; as to splatter dashes, none of the soldiers have received any. I must tell you that every soldier who has received these, has paid for them. So that you may assure your company there is no distinction made.

"If you have one Halbert, it is more than we have in the whole regiment; and I desire it may be laid aside, and a musket etc. substituted in its place. Cartridge paper is an article not to be had here; and we make use of horns and pouches in its stead." (*Writings* - 2 - Pages 102-103)

Note: A "splatter dash" was apparently a short legging and a "halbert" is defined by Webster as "a kind of long handled weapon, especially in use in the 15th and 16th centuries." The use of the latter as a practical threat to the Indians on the frontier of western Virginia in 1757 seems ludicrous in the extreme.

September, 1758 — Petition of Doctor Henry Heath

"Petition of Doctor Henry Heath, setting forth that he attended the drafted soldiers at Winchester in their sickness, by order of the Commanding Officer 50 days, for which and his medicines and advice he charges 25 Pounds and that he has only received 10 Pounds and 10 shillings

34

and praying to be paid the balance by the public." (*Journal House of Burgesses* - 1758 - Page 32)

Hospital in Winchester — Petition of Benjamin Grub

"A petition of Benjamin Grub of the Town of Winchester, setting forth that in the spring of the year 1755 the petitioner's house in the said Town was by order of Col. Stephen, Commanding Officer of the Virginia troops then stationed there, taken and converted into a hospital for the use of the soldiers, who kept possession thereof for that purpose about eight months, and during that time destroying the paling of the lot on which the house stood entirely, and the plastering of the house, ripped off the boards of the dwelling house and stable, and did the petitioner other considerable damage valued by workmen to above forty pounds, for which Sir John St. Clair, to whom the petitioner delivered the estimate, promised to procure an allowance. But the petitioner has never heard anything more of it, nor received any satisfaction for the use of the house, or injury done him by the Soldiers." (*Journal of House of Burgesses* 1766-69 - Page 162)

Note: This building stood on Lot Number 9 on the west side of South Loudoun Street, just south of the Cocks property where Col. Washington lived. It was granted originally to Thomas Wood (*Props. Grants* - Book N - Page 326) who sold it on December 11, 1756 to Benjamin Grub. (*F.D.B.* - 4 - Page 187). In modern location terms the building stood about where the Palace Theater lot is. The date of the acquisition of the lot by Grubb leads us to believe that the date in the petition may be in error.

The account book of Col. Washington with the Colony of Virginia for the 1755-1758 period contains the names of a number of Winchester residents with whom the Colonel conducted business for the Colony. This account book is now in the manuscripts division of the Library of Congress and we are recording as follows some of the entries which we think may be of interest to our readers:

October 15, 1755 — Paid John Campbell for making ramrods.

October 18, 1755 — Paid William Mungars, smith, for repairing arms

October 21, 1755 — Paid George Wright, smith, for repairing arms.

October 24, 1755 — Paid Tim Higgins, smith, for repairing arms.

December 3, 1755 — Paid Alexander Kennedy for a ton of Iron.

December 22, 1755 — Paid Joseph Perry for taking care of Carolina Beeves.

December 29, 1755 — Paid William Mungars, smith, for making and mending Handcuffs.

January, 2, 1756 — Paid Patrick Leyden's wife sundries and cutting wood.

January 6, 1756 — Paid Dr. Watson his account of medicines furnished sick.

January 6, 1756 — Paid Edward Snickers wagonage from Alexandria to Winchester.

January 9, 1756 — Paid Mary Bailey nurse to Hospital at Winchester.

April 15, 1756 — Paid Thomas Kirkpatrick for 200 pr. Stockings.

April 27, 1756 — Paid John Butler for bringing 2 casks of powder from Fredericksburg.

May 6, 1756 — Paid Owen Jenkins for making handcuffs.

May 6, 1756 — Paid Daniel Hiver and Carpenters for building a breastwork round the Court House in defense of the Town.

May 8, 1756 — Paid Godfrey Humbert for making a coffin for a soldier.

May 12, 1756 — Paid David Deadrick for skins to make drumheads.

May 13, 1756 — Paid John Greenfield for moccasins for Nottoway Indians.

May 15, 1756 — Paid Griffith Evans for repairing and strengthening arms.

May 21, 1756 — Paid for Drum cords and other necessaries for the drums.

June 2, 1756 — Paid John Dow for 8½ barrels of corn for the troops.

June 3, 1756 — Paid for Cord to make caps for the drummers.

June 16, 1756 — Paid James Allen for making a military chest.

June 17, 1756 — Paid John Mitchell for 200 pairs of men's shoes.

June 27, 1756 — Paid Helverstone (Helphinstine) and Otto for 41 pairs of shoes.

June 28, 1756 — Paid Philip Bush funeral expenses for Henry Campbell.

  Note: The Proprietor of the Golden Buck was apparently also an undertaker.

July 12, 1756 — Paid Peter Stalker for rum for the use of the soldiers.

July 14, 1756 — Paid John Frazer for cleaning and repairing arms.

August 10, 1756 — Paid Nottoway Indians for their expenses homeward.

August 20, 1756 — Paid Dr. Craik for purchasing medicine.
   Note: Dr. Craik was associated with Washington for many years and attended him in his last illness.

August 29, 1756 — Paid a Dutchman for a bucket to the well.
   Note: No doubt the well at Fort Loudoun.

September 6, 1756 — Paid Mr. Jones, Lawyer's fee about Tippling Houses.
   Note: This was Gabriel Jones, the King's Attorney and Washington's close friend who acted for him against the "tippling house" or keeper's in Winchester who sold intoxicants against the Colonel's orders.

October 6, 1756 — Paid Kate Kennison, nurse at the Hospital.
   Note: This is one of a number of records of payments to Kate Kennison.

December 9, 1756 — Paid Henry Heth for pasturage and sundry expenses.

December 18, 1756 — Paid Thomas Worthington for buckskins for the Cherokees.

January 1, 1757 — Paid Jacob Seabrat (Siebert or Seabright) for buckskins for the Catawbas.

April 1, 1757 — "Paid Christian Heintz in part for digging well in Fort Loudoun." Note: This is one of a number of payments to Heintz for digging the Fort Loudoun well: For example July 5, 1757 — To Christopher Heintz - well digger; August 27, 1757 — To John Christian Heintz - well digger; October 7, 1757 — To John Christopher Heintz - well digger; April 22, 1758 — To John Christopher Heintz - for working in barracks yard 16 days in blowing rock - digging 48 feet in well of Fort Loudoun."

April 20, 1757 — Paid John Greenfield for 3 match coats for Tuscaroras.

June 29, 1757 — Paid Daniel Jennings for riding express to Fairfax County Lieutenant in order to stop the militia from marching to Winchester upon the alarm of the French and Indians coming against Fort Cumberland.

July 5, 1757 — Paid Isaac Parkins for 2 barrels of beer to Cherokee Indians.

July 13, 1757 — Paid Jackson & Fitzsimmons their charge for burning lime.

August 5, 1757 — Paid Edmond Atkins Esq. for 70 duffle, blankets for soldiers.

August 20, 1757 — Paid John Patterson for overseeing the workers at Fort Loudoun from 30 November, 1756 to the 10th of December.

August 27, 1757 — Paid Benj. Tomlinson for securing 5 sheep skins for cannon sponges.

August 30, 1757 — Paid Joshua Baker Armorer for work to date.

August 31, 1757 — Paid David Datry (Dietrich) for 5 sheep skins to make spunges.

September 1, 1757 — Paid Christian Neitzell for making two hundred straps and frogs for the detachment sent to Carolina under Col. Stephens.

September 1, 1757 — Paid Henry Rinker for making 227 scabbards for detachments sent to Carolina.

September 1, 1757 — Paid Nathaniel Cartmell for horse hire.

September 17, 1757 — Paid Henry Carter for horse hire to escort the Cherokees.

June 1, 1758 — Paid Fielding Lewis for nails.

June 1, 1758 — Paid John Greenafield for hospital rent.

June 1, 1758 — Paid James Craik, Surgeon.

June 18, 1758 — Paid Mr. Franks of Philadelphia for leggins for 1st Virginia Regiment.

Washington also kept a personal account book during this period, to which reference has already been made in this study. This book is also preserved in the Library of Congress. This account book among other entries shows that: he gave a soldier's wife 5 shillings on April 14, 1756; that he gave a crippled man 5 shillings on April 16, 1756; that he paid a Doctor Watson 5 shillings for drawing a tooth on April 27, 1756; that he "gave a man who had his house burnt" a pound on May 25, 1756; that he paid Dutch Cowper an unspecified amount "for a puppy" on December 10, 1756; that he paid "for billiards" one shilling and 10½ pence (whether for a gambling loss in the game or for the cost of playing we do not know). These entries are recorded here to show that George Washington, in addition to being a great and wise leader, was a very human and considerate man who could buy a puppy in the midst of his heavy responsibilities, or play a game of billiards, or give a pound to a poor settler whose house had been burnt perhaps by marauding savages.

Washington ran for public office the first time in Winchester and was elected for the first time. In all he ran three times for the office of Burgess from Frederick County: in 1755, 1758, and 1761. The first time he was defeated; the other two times he was elected.

Frederick County was entitled to two Burgesses. In the term immediately preceding 1755 the original Burgesses were George William Fairfax and Gabriel Jones. Jones, however, resigned in 1754, and Isaac Parkins was chosen to fill his unexpired term. (*Journal House of B.* 1752-58 - Page 167). By 1755 Parkins decided not to remain in office, and George William Fairfax resigned to become a candidate in Fairfax County. Hugh West and Thomas Swearingin immediately declared for the offices. On the very day of the election, December 10, 1755, some of Col. Washington's friends presented his name for the position, but they had made no previous canvass, and it appears doubtful that they even informed him of what they intended to do. The result of the election was that Hugh West received 271 votes; Thomas Swearingin 270 votes; and Washington 40 votes. (816 *Papers of Washington* - Library of Congress)

There has long been a tradition in Winchester that Washington lost this election because he had alienated the support of the "tippling house keepers" or ordinary keepers in Winchester, particularly of one Lindsay, the renewal of whose license Washington had opposed. Dr. Freeman in his definitive life of Washington discounts this allegation, quoting Robert Barton as follows: "If this hostility did exist, it could not have shown itself until election-day because the candidacy of the commander was not known till then." (*Freeman* - Vol. 2 - Page 147 - Note 162) We might add that Washington's difficulties with the "tippling house" keepers came principally after this date, and we can conclude that his defeat was due to the fact that he was a newcomer whose friends had not allowed the time for a proper canvass, rather than from the influence of the liquor interests.

In connection with the discussion of Washington's election to the House of Burgesses it seems to us appropriate to explain the procedures by which one became a Burgess. In the first place two Burgesses from each County had to be chosen by a plurality of the qualified voters of the County. A qualified voter had to be a white male 21 years of age who during one whole year had been the bona fide owner of at least one hundred acres of land not settled upon or of twenty-five acres "with a house and plantation" in his possession or occupied by a tenant, in the County in which he voted; in a town established by the Assembly, the ownership of a house and lot. (*Hening* 4 - Page 475) The voting took place at the Court House in the presence of the Sheriff and Justices of the Peace and the Candidates or their proxies. Clerks of each candidate were also present with a poll sheet to record the vote. Voters would approach the table where the officials were assembled and when their names were called out they vocally announced their choice and the candidates bowed and thanked the voters for their support. The presence of the candidate at the poll was highly desirable from his standpoint, but he could have a proxy to represent him, as we shall presently see.

Remembering the experience of 1755, Washington announced early his candidacy for the House of Burgesses from Frederick County, which would be decided at an election to be held on July 24, 1758. Unfortunately it early became apparent that military duty at Fort Cumberland would keep him out of Winchester on the day of the election and the period immediately preceding it.

Col. Thomas Bryan Martin, nephew of Lord Fairfax, who had been a Burgess from Hampshire County, decided to contest for Hugh West's seat from Frederick; and Washington was left to challenge Thomas Swearingen.

The friends of Washington, realizing that military necessity might keep him away from Frederick County even on the day of the election, pitched in to help him. George William Fairfax and John Carlyle agreed to visit old Frederick and to see to it that their tenants supported the Colonel. (*Hamilton* 2 - Page 343). James Wood, the founder of Winchester, Clerk of the Frederick County Court, and probably the most influential man in the County, backed Washington solidly and was his proxy at the canvass. Gabriel Jones, the Kings Attorney, and a Burgess from Augusta County neglected his own race in order to campaign for his young friend. Lieut. Charles Smith, in command at Fort Loudoun when Washington was absent, was his campaign manager and kept him informed of the progress of the race. (*Hamilton* - 2 - Page 397)

To understand why Washington's presence was so necessary at Fort Cumberland about this time we must point out, as we have not previously done, that by 1758 the British Government had decided on a new attack upon Fort Duquesne. Over strenuous objections from Washington and other Virginia leaders, who thought the road to the French fort should be by the already-cleared Braddock Road, it had been decided to cut a new road, all in the Colony of Pennsylvania, from Philadelphia by way of Carlisle, Shippensburg, Raystown and Loyal Hannon. Brigadier General John Forbes had been selected to head this expedition, and his second-in-command was Lieut.-Col. Henry Bouquet. The forces under Washington's command would be expected to join this effort whenever the order was given. Col. Bouquet, who was Washington's immediate superior, seems to have been willing to allow the young Virginian to go to Winchester for the election on July 24, but finally on July 19 Washington settled the matter in a letter to Bouquet when he stated that he had decided "rather to leave the management of (the polling) to the care of my friends than to be absent from my Regiment when there is a probability of its being called upon." (*Writings* - 2 - Page 242) So the canvass went on without the candidate's presence in this case.

A letter from Lieut. Charles Smith from Fort Loudoun to Washington on July 26, 1758 contained "a true copy of the Poll whereby you will be a compitent judge of your friends". (*Hamilton* - 2 - Page 298) This copy revealed that the vote was: Washington - 209; Martin - 239; West - 199; Swearingen - 45. So Washington and Martin became the new Burgesses from Frederick County. This letter also revealed that Smith had purchased for Washington 28 gallons of rum; 50 gallons of rum punch; 34 gallons of wine; 46 gallons of Beer; and 2 gallons of Cider Royal, which had been consumed by the voters on election day. The total bill to the Colonel for this liquor and dinner for his especial friends was 39 Pounds and 6 shillings.

Washington had not been there to join in the celebration, but his proxy, Col. James Wood, received the honor of being chaired through the streets of Winchester in his stead. A familiar picture of this incident appeared first in Graham's Magazine in 1853. (*Greene* - Page 97)

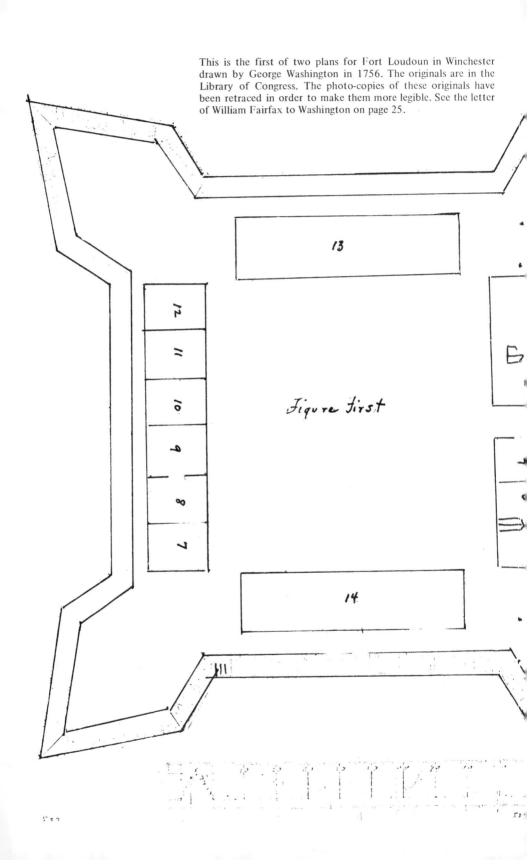

This is the first of two plans for Fort Loudoun in Winchester drawn by George Washington in 1756. The originals are in the Library of Congress. The photo-copies of these originals have been retraced in order to make them more legible. See the letter of William Fairfax to Washington on page 25.

13

12

11

10

9

8

7

Figure first

14

E

Figure first

Represents the Walls of the Fort the Houses, and other conveniences upon & above the Ramparts.

A B - is the Width of the Rampart after the Parapet and Banquette is taken off

B C - is the width of the Banquette.

C.D - is the width of the parapet and

A C - is the width of the passage round the houses ___ from the ___ to the parapet story may be seen more plainly on Figure 2, Line BO.

Bastion No 1 will be the powder Magazine The Sd. Bastion will be roofed or covered over to become a passage for the convenience of the defenders to pass to and fro Across the Gorge No 2 is en Office. Nos. 3 & 4 is conveniency rooms No 5 is a bed Chamber No 6 is a dining Room No 7, 8, 9, 10, 11, 12 are apartments for officers No 13 & 14 may be formed into store rooms, an hospital, Chappel, Barracks or &c as occasion may require

To Winchester abt 200 Yards

Figure Second

Shews in perspective, a view of the House wall

AB - is ye width of the House and rooms exclusive of the passage
AO - with the passage the width
BO - is the width of the passage
BD - the width of ye Rampart at the top
BE - the width at bottom
DE - the Taper or slope
OD - the thickness of the parapet
OP - the Height
EF -
FH - the width of ditch at top
GM - Do at the Bottom
FG & HM the taper of the ditch
AI & HN the depth of the Ditch
IK the height of the wall & first story of the houses
KL Height of the second story of Do.

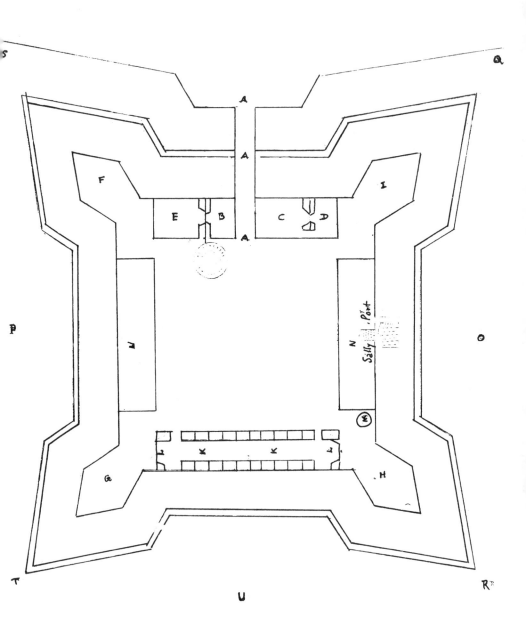

This is the second of two plans for Fort Loudoun in Winchester drawn
by George Washington in 1756. (See comment on first plan)

The Ground Work of the Fort

A. Is the way into It.

B. Is the Officers Guard Room.

C. Soldiers Ditto

D. Prison

E. A Kitchen

F. Powder Magazine.

G. H. I. Magazine for Provisions

K. K. Soldiers Barracks - two tiers

L. L. Two Large Fire Places for Cooking

M. The Well

N. N. Two large Houses to be converted into Barracks, Store Houses as occasion shall require.

N. B. The Gate of the Fort fronts the main Street in Winchester & is distant abt' 150 or 200 yards from the Town and abt' 40 feet higher, with a gradual descent all the way. On the sides O & P. are deep valleys which come up to the points of the Bastions at Q. R. & S. T. especially on the side O from whence on a hill at abt' 100 yds distance, which forms a second valley and cover for the enemy to approach under, we have the greatest reason to apprehend an attack. On the side U is but little fall & quite regular.

In October, 1758 Washington was ordered to march his troops to join the Forbes expedition, and from that time until the conclusion of the slow and tedious march to Fort Duquesne participated vigorously in the movement. On the night of November 24, while the Forbes forces were encamped near the site of Braddock's defeat in 1755, a tremendous explosion was heard. The next day the English and American troops reached Fort Duquesne to find that the French had blown up the fort and departed, leaving to Forbes an empty victory. Some time prior to this the French had captured a number of the members of the 77th Highlander Regiment, which comprised the bulk of the Forbes army. As the British approached the fort on November 25 they found the road lined on each side by posts on whose tops were the heads of these captured Highlanders; and below were lashed their kilts.

The fall of Fort Duquesne removed to a major degree the threat to the Virginia frontier, and Washington, looking forward to his coming marriage and believing that his job for the Virginia Colony was completed, assigned some of the men of the First Virginia Regiment to garrison duty at the captured fort, and hurried homeward. He arrived in Winchester on December 8 sick and exhausted, and near the end of the month after partial recuperation rode on to *Belvoir*. (*Writings* - 2 - Page 317) Thus came to an end the ten year period of his intimate and rather continuous association with Winchester.

We should mention the fact that in the election of Burgesses for Frederick County held on May 18, 1761 Washington was again a candidate, and on this occasion he apparently canvassed the area thoroughly. In a letter to Captain Van Swearingen from Frederick County on Friday May 15, 1761, he has the following to say about the coming election and about his own preparation for it:

> "At the cock fight on Saturday I promised to be at a wedding at Mendenhall's Mills yesterday, which together with an affair I had to settle on Bullskin (That detained me a day longer than I expected) prevented my taking Shepherds Town and your house in my way. I intend this day to pass along the North Mountain and tomorrow at ten at a meeting at McGills on the Cumberland Road and from thence to Winchester in order to wait my doom on Mon-

day." (From a letter in private hands quoted in *Fitzpatrick* - Page 155)

The candidates in the election were Washington, George Mercer, and Adam Stephen and a number of minor last-minute aspirants. The poll of May 18 gave Washington 505 votes, Mercer 399, and Stephen 294. During Washington's stay in Winchester on this occasion he stopped at Philip Bush's Inn. (*Writings* - 2 - Note Page 359)

During his terms as Burgess from Frederick County we can find only one bit of legislation affecting the Town of Winchester, which he sponsored. The Journal of the House of Burgesses for March 1, 1761 (Page 228) records that

"Mr. Washington presented to the House, according to order, a bill to prevent hogs running at large within the Town of Winchester or the limits thereof."

He continued as Burgess from Frederick until July 16, 1765. A vacancy had occurred in Fairfax County and he, therefore, sought a seat nearer home, where it would be easier for him to make a canvass and announced for the vacancy, at the same time declining election in Frederick. He won the election and became a Fairfax Burgess, which position he held for many years. (*Papers of Washington* Library of Congress - 816).

Washington was in Winchester a number of times after 1758 for short visits, but in the aggregate the decade from 1748 to 1758 was the time when he was here most frequently. Several years ago there was a Broadway hit comedy with the title *Washington Slept Here*. Its theme was based upon the all-too-frequent American past-time of trying to capitalize upon the fact that the Father of our Country by some myopic view of history may have spent a night in a dwelling which they owned. Fortunately Winchester does not have to resort to such hypocrisy. She can, we believe, document the fact that Washington slept more nights in Winchester than in any other place away from home, excepting New York and Philadelphia, where he lived when he was President. Washington did indeed sleep in this old Virginia town many, many times.

APPENDIX

Result of Poll for Burgesses from Frederick County Held in Winchester, December 10, 1755

(From Photocopy of Manuscript in Library of Congress)

Col. George Washington	Capt. Thomas Swearingen	Mr. Hugh West
. . . .	Isaac Parkins	Isaac Parkins
. . . .	Lawrence Stephens	Lawrence Stephens
James Brown	. . . .	James Brown
. . . .	Thomas Hampton	Thomas Hampton
. . . .	John White	John White
. . . .	John Evans	John Evans
. . . .	William Gaddes	William Gaddes
Ryley Moore	Ryley Moore	. . . .
. . . .	Andrew Caldwell	Andrew Caldwell
. . . .	John Jones	John Jones
. . . .	William Jolleff	William Jolleff
. . . .	Robert Halfpenny	Robert Halfpenny
. . . .	David Osborn	David Osborn
. . . .	Richard Mercer	Richard Mercer
Magnus Tate	Magnus Tate	. . . .
. . . .	William Nealy	William Nealy
Reuben Pritchett	. . . .	Reuben Pritchett
Valentine Crawford	Valentine Crawford	. . . .
. . . .	William Davis	William Davis
. . . .	David Vance	David Vance
. . . .	Robert Rayborn	Robert Rayborn
. . . .	Edward Cartmel	Edward Cartmel
Alexander Matthews	Alexander Matthews	. . . .
. . . .	Joseph Langdon	Joseph Langdon
. . . .	John Shearer	John Shearer
. . . .	Henry Vanmeter	Henry Vanmeter
. . . .	Thomas Doster	Thomas Doster
. . . .	Joseph Horner	Joseph Horner
. . . .	Samuel Stroud	Samuel Stroud
. . . .	John Chinnoeth	John Chinnoeth
John Calvey	John Calvey	. . . .
. . . .	Samuel Parks	Samuel Parks
Robert Pearis	Robert Pearis	. . . .
. . . .	James Hoges	James Hoges
. . . .	Henry Histant (?)	Henry Histant (?)
. . . .	Leonard Helm	Leonard Helm
. . . .	James McGill	James McGill
. . . .	Zebulon Hollingsworth	Zebulon Hollingworth
. . . .	Thomas Babb	Thomas Babb
. . . .	David Shephard	David Shephard
. . . .	Robert Glass	Robert Glass
Alexander Vance	Alexander Vance	. . . .
. . . .	Nicholas Lemon	Nicholas Lemon
. . . .	Jeremiah Cloud	Jeremiah Cloud
Van Swearingen	Van Swearingen	. . . .

Washington	Swearingen	West
. . . .	Samuel Blackburn	Samuel Blackburn
. . . .	Edward Dodd	Edward Dodd
. . . .	Benjamin Blackburn	Benjamin Blackburn
. . . .	Hugh Lyles	Hugh Lyles
. . . .	James Cromley	James Cromley
. . . .	Melchior Engles	Melchior Engles
. . . .	William Stroop	William Stroop
. . . .	George Bowman	George Bowman
. . . .	Daniel Johnson	Daniel Johnson
. . . .	Stephen Southwood	Stephen Southwood
. . . .	Edward Black	Edward Black
. . . .	James Gatlet	James Gatlet
. . . .	Thomas Chester	Thomas Chester
. . . .	John Snapp, Jr.	John Snapp, Jr.
. . . .	James Blair	James Blair
William McKee	William McKee	. . . .
. . . .	Benjamin Grub	Benjamin Grub
. . . .	Joseph McDowels	Joseph McDowels
. . . .	Richard Morgan	Richard Morgan
. . . .	John Lemon	John Leomon
William Calmes	. . . .	William Calmes
. . . .	Nathaniel Bell	Nathaniel Bell
. . . .	Evan Thomas	Evan Thomas
. . . .	John Thomas	John Thomas
. . . .	Jacob Vanmeter	Jacob Vanmeter
. . . .	Hugh Devenny	Hugh Devenny
William Cochran	William Cochran	. . . .
. . . .	Edward Lindsay	Edward Lindsay
John McCormick	. . . .	John McCormick
Richard Stephenson	. . . .	Richard Stephenson
. . . .	John Strickler	John Strickler
. . . .	Enos Thomas	Enos Thomas
. . . .	Morris Reeves	Morris Reeves
. . . .	William Roberts	William Roberts
. . . .	Jacob Barkinghall	Jacob Barkinghall
Robert Rutherford	. . . .	Robert Rutherford
Taliaferro Stribling	. . . .	Taliaferro Stribling
Adam Hunter	. . . .	Adam Hunter
. . . .	William Lupton	William Lupton
Nicholas Princeller	. . . .	Nicholas Princeller
. . . .	Ellis Thomas	Ellis Thomas
. . . .	Robert Cunningham	Robert Cunningham
. . . .	Capt. John Denton	Capt. John Denton
. . . .	Samuel Denton	Samuel Denton
. . . .	Robert Lemon	Robert Lemon
. . . .	Alexander Oglesby	Alexander Oglesby
. . . .	Peter Foster	Peter Foster
William Bethal	. . . .	William Bethal
. . . .	William Roberts Jr.	William Roberts Jr.
. . . .	David Etrick	David Etrick
. . . .	John (Haddle, Handal)	John (Haddle, Handal)
. . . .	Charles (Howels, Huddles)	Charles (Howels, Huddles)
. . . .	Christopher Beelar	Christopher Beelar
. . . .	John Funkhouser	John Funkhouser

Washington	Swearingen	West
. . . .	John Snapp	John Snapp
. . . .	Abraham Vanmeter	Abraham Vanmeter
. . . .	Robert Paul	Robert Paul
. . . .	Phillip Glass	Phillip Glass
. . . .	Robert Edwards	Robert Edwards
. . . .	Bernard Sibert	Bernard Sibert
. . . .	David Lewis	David Lewis
. . . .	Paul Froman	Paul Froman
. . . .	Peter Wolfe	Peter Wolfe
. . . .	William Burn	William Burn
. . . .	Peter Houghman	Peter Houghman
. . . .	William Heth	William Heth
. . . .	Daniel Holman	Daniel Holman
. . . .	Benjamin Thornbury	Benjamin Thornbury
. . . .	Ribhard McMachen	Richard McMachen
. . . .	Thomas Mason	Thomas Mason
. . . .	Robert Fulsom	Robert Fulsom
. . . .	Abraham Fry	Abraham Fry
. . . .	William Moore	William Moore
. . . .	David Melon	David Melon
. . . .	Jeremiah Smith	Jeremiah Smith
. . . .	Henry Loyd	Henry Loyd
. . . .	George Pemberton	George Pemberton
. . . .	William Baldwin	William Baldwin
Robert Ashby	. . . .	Robert Ashby
. . . .	George Ross	George Ross
. . . .	William Chennowith	William Chennowith
. . . .	John Hiat	John Hiat
. . . .	Peter Rufover (?)	Peter Rufover (?)
. . . .	Christian Houghman	Christian Houghman
. . . .	John Naffe	John Naffe
. . . .	Andrew Paul	Andrew Paul
. . . .	Thomas Thornbury	Thomas Thornbury
. . . .	Isaac Evans	Isaac Evans
. . . .	Aaron Jenkins	Aaron Jenkins
. . . .	John Vance	. . . .
. . . .	Andrew Vance	Andrew Vance
. . . .		Samuel Vance
. . . .	Joseph Parrel	Joseph Parrel
. . . .	John Tewalt	John Tewalt
. . . .	John Small	John Small
. . . .	Edward Mercer Jr.	. . . .
. . . .	Isaac Ruddles	Isaac Ruddles
. . . .	Edward Teague	Edward Teague
. . . .	John Borden	John Borden
. . . .	William Hall	William Hall
. . . .	Abraham Brubaker	Abraham Brubaker
. . . .	Sameul Littler	Samuel Littler
. . . .	John Miller	John Miller
. . . .	John Blackburn (?)	. . . .
. . . .	Charles Baker	Charles Baker
. . . .	William Spurgen	William Spurgen
. . . .	John Hiat Jr.	John Hiat Jr.
. . . .	Anthony Turner	Anthony Turner
. . . .	Anthony Turner Jr.	Anthony Turner Jr.

46

Washington	Swearingen	West
. . . .	Gersham Keys	Gersham Keys
. . . .	Rev. John Gordon	Rev. John Gordon
. . . .	John Vestal	John Vestal
. . . .	Isaac Pemberton	Isaac Pemberton
Elisha Parkins	Elisha Parkins	. . . .
. . . .	Robert Marney	Robert Marney
. . . .	Samuel Patten	Samuel Patten
. . . .	James Colvin	James Colvin
. . . .	William Evans	William Evans
. . . .	Nicholas Handshires	Nicholas Handshires
. . . .	Patrick Rice	Patrick Rice
. . . .	Samuel Isaacs	Samuel Isaacs
. . . .	George Hampton	George Hampton
. . . .	Joseph Colvin	Joseph Colvin
. . . .	John Mendinghall	John Mendinghall
. . . .	Thomas Butler	Thomas Butler
. . . .	Josiah Ballinger	Josiah Ballinger
. . . .	Jacob Moon	Jacob Moon
. . . .	George Henry	George Henry
. . . .	Samuel Pearson	Samuel Pearson
Col. James Wood	. . . .	Col. James Wood
. . . .	William Frost	William Frost
. . . .	Harry Pifer (?)	Harry Pifer (?)
. . . .	Henry Kockenal	Henry Kockendal
. . . .	(Kuykendahl)	(Kuykendahl)
. . . .	Jacob Christman	Jacob Christman
. . . .	George Sellar	George Sellar
. . . .	Christopher Windles	Christopher Windles
. . . .	Adam Funk	Adam Funk
. . . .	Henry Stephen	Henry Stephen
. . . .	Jacob Gibson	Jacob Gibson
. . . .	Joseph Glass	Joseph Glass
. . . .	Ulrich Stoner	Ulrich Stoner
John Briscoe	. . . .	John Briscoe
. . . .	John Limback	John Limback
. . . .	Joseph Lupton	Joseph Lupton
. . . .	Peter Stephen	Peter Stephen
. . . .	Jacob Pursols	Jacob Pursols
William Russell	. . . .	William Russell
. . . .	Samuel Bean	. . . .
. . . .	Peter Stover	. . . .
. . . .	George Huddles	George Huddles
. . . .	George Mowrey	. . . .
. . . .	John Milburn	John Milburn
. . . .	Jacob Reece	Jacob Reece
. . . .	Christian Grabil	Christian Grabil
. . . .	Andrew Longacre	Andrew Lonacre
. . . .	Richard Faucet	Richard Faucet
. . . .	Martin Feugates	Martin Feugates
. . . .	Reynolds Bodgins	Raynolds Bodgins
. . . .	(Baldwin)	(Baldwin)
. . . .	Lewis Smalthousen	Lewis Smalthousen
. . . .	Francis Lyllbourn	Francis Lyllbourn
. . . .	Joseph Dunham	Joseph Dunham
. . . .	Otho Peters	Otho Peters

Washington	Swearingen	West
. . . .	Patrick Dunham	Patrick Dunham
. . . .	John Grabil	John Grabil
. . . .	John Blank	John Blank
. . . .	William Dougherty	William Dougherty
. . . .	Jeremiah Stroud	Jeremiah Stroud
. . . .	John Thomas	John Thomas
. . . .	Valentine Windles	Valentine Windles
. . . .	Michael Baker	Michael Baker
. . . .	John Beckets	John Beckets
. . . .	John Nisewanger	John Nisewanger
. . . .	Owen Rogers	Owen Rogers
Henry Moore	. . . .	Henry Moore
. . . .	Jesse Peugh (Pugh)	Jesse Peugh (Pugh)
. . . .	William Hust (?)	William Hust (?)
. . . .	Joseph Fry	Joseph Fry
William Potter	. . . .	William Potter
. . . .	Ralph Withers	Ralph Withers
. . . .	Martin Grider	Martin Grider
. . . .	Joseph Roberts	Joseph Roberts
. . . .	Jarvice Daugherty	Jarvice Daugherty
Thomas Wadlington	. . . .	Thomas Wadlington
Edward Lonaggars	. . . .	Edward Lonaggars
(Longacres)	. . . .	(Longacres)
. . . .	Matthias Funk	Matthias Funk
. . . .	Francis Baldwin	Francis Baldwin
. . . .	John Skeen	John Skeen
. . . .	Isaac Beeson	Isaac Beeson
. . . .	Thomas Lindsey	Thomas Lindsey
. . . .	John Davis	John Davis
Joseph Borden	. . . .	Joseph Borden
. . . .	Christopher Marr	Christopher Marr
. . . .	Robert Stockdon	Robert Stockdon
. . . .	John Reed	John Reed
. . . .	David Right (Wright)	David Right (Wright)
. . . .	Reuben Paxton (?)	Reuben Paxton (?)
. . . .	Phillip Babb	Phillip Babb
. . . .	Morgan Morgan	Morgan Morgan
. . . .	William Dillon	William Dillon
Henry Heth	. . . .	Henry Heth
. . . .	Thomas Low	Thomas Low
. . . .	Nathaniel Cartmell	Nathaniel Cartmell
. . . .	Agariah Peugh (Pugh)	Agariah Peugh (Pugh)
Thomas Perry	. . . .	Thomas Perry
. . . .	James Night (Knight)	James Night (Knight)
. . . .	William White	William White
. . . .	Frederick Grider (Crider	Frederick Grider (Crider)
. . . .	Jacob Sowers	Jacob Sowers
. . . .	Richard Highland	Richard Highland
. . . .	Simeon Linder	Simeon Linder
. . . .	Richard Sturman	Richard Sturman
Edward Cordrey	. . . .	Edward Cordrey
. . . .	David Glass	David Glass
. . . .	Dennis Bow	Dennis Bow
. . . .	Edward Thomas	Edward Thomas
. . . .	Reese Pritchard	Reese Pritchard

48

Washington	Swearingen	West
. . . .	Jacob Cooper	Jacob Cooper
. . . .	George Dellinger	George Dellinger
. . . .	John Hopes	John Hopes
Augustine Windle	Augustine Windle	. . . .
. . . .	George Hollingsworth	George Hollingsworth
. . . .	James Carter	James Carter
. . . .	Robert Calvert	Robert Calvert
. . . .	Harrison Taylor	Harrison Taylor
. . . .	John Fewel	John Fewel
. . . .	William Reynalls	William Reynalls
. . . .	(Reynolds)	(Reynolds)
. . . .	Joseph Wilkerson	Joseph Wilkerson
. . . .	Robert Worthington	Robert Worthington
Robert Worthington Jr.	Robert Worthington Jr.	. . . .
. . . .	John Maddin	John Maddin
. . . .	Robert McCoy	Robert McCoy
. . . .	Abraham Haines	Abraham Haines
. . . .	Darby Murphey	Darby Murphey
. . . .	Martin Funk	Martin Funk
William Crawford	William Crawford	. . . .
. . . .	William Barrets	William Barrets
. . . .	Isaac Hollingsworth	Isaac Hollingsworth
. . . .	William Helm	William Helm
. . . .	Dennis Springer	Dennis Springer
. . . .	Thomas Colson	Thomas Colson
. . . .	Charles Parkins	Charles Parkins
. . . .	Nathan Cartmell	Nathan Cartmell
Henry Brinker	. . . .	Henry Brinker
. . . .	Robert Allen	Robert Allen
Meredith Helm	Meredith Helm	. . . .
Thomas Helm	Thomas Helm	. . . .
. . . .	Charles Buck	. . . .
. . . .	Lewis Stephen	Lewis Stephen
James Lemon	James Lemon	

Result of Poll for Burgesses from Frederick County Held in Winchester July 24, 1758

(From Washington Manuscript Library of Congress, Alphabetized in Hamilton II—p. 401)

Col. George Washington	Col. Thomas Bryan Martin	Mr. Hugh West	Capt. Thomas Swearingen
Robert Ashby	Robert Ashby	. . . .	. . . .
Thomas A	Thomas Ashby	. . . .	. . . .
Robert Allan	Robert Allan	. . . .	. . . .
John Ashby	John Ashby	. . . .	. . . .
Stephen Ashby	Stephen Ashby	. . . .	. . . .
Rev. John Alderson	Rev. John Alderson	. . . .	. . . .
. . . .	John Armstrong	John Armstrong	. . . .
John Allan (Taylor)	. . . .		. . . .
John Arnold	. . . .	John Arnold	. . . .
. . . .	. . . .	John Anderson	John Anderson
James Burn	James Burn	. . . .	. . . .
Dennis Bow	Dennis Bow	. . . .	. . . .
Christopher Beiler		Christopher Beiler	. . . .
Andrew Blackburn	Andrew Blackburn	. . . .	. . . .
James Ballenger	. . . .	James Ballenger	. . . .
Jacob Burner	Jacob Burner	. . . .	. . . .
John Bombgardner	John Bombgardner	. . . .	. . . .
Samuel Blackburn	Samuel Blackburn	. . . .	. . . .
Thomas Babb	. . . .	Thomas Babb	. . . .
Charles Baker	Charles Baker	. . . .	. . . .
Samuel Beam	Samuel Beam	. . . .	. . . .
Reynald Baldwin	Reynald Baldwin	. . . .	. . . .
Richard Barber	Richard Barber	. . . .	. . . .
John Blair	John Blair	. . . .	. . . .
Jacob Bowman	Jacob Bowman	. . . .	. . . .
George Bower	George Bower	. . . .	. . . .
Henry Biber	Henry Biber	. . . .	. . . .
Martin Black	Martin Black	. . . .	. . . .
Philip Babb	. . . .	Philip Babb	. . . .
James Burne	James Burne	. . . .	. . . .
William Baldwin	. . . .	William Baldwin	. . . .
Joseph Burden	. . . .	Joseph Burden	. . . .
James Blair	. . . .	James Blair	. . . .
Henry Brinker	Henry Brinker	. . . .	. . . .
Charles Barnes	Charles Barnes	. . . .	. . . .
James Barret	. . . .	James Barret	. . . .
William Barret	. . . .	William Barret	. . . .
John Briscoe	. . . .	John Briscoe	. . . .
Thomas Babb	. . . .	Thomas Babb	. . . .
(son of Philip)	. . . .	(son of Philip)	. . . .
George Bruce	. . . .	George Burce	. . . .
Henry Bowen	. . . .	Henry Bowen	. . . .
Thomas Babb Jr.	. . . .	Thomas Babb Jr.	. . . .
Peter Babb	. . . .	Peter Babb	. . . .
Joseph Babb	. . . .	Joseph Babb	. . . .

Washington	Martin	West	Swearingen
Bryan Bruin	Bryan Bruin	. . . .	. . . .
John Buckley	John Buckley	. . . .	. . . .
Jacob Barret	. . . .	Jacob Barret	. . . .
Joshua Baker .	. . . .	Joshua Baker	
. . . .	Tobias Burk	Tobias Burk	. . . .
John Bentley	John Bentley	. . . .	. . . .
. . . .	John Burden	. . . .	John Burden
. . . .	George Bowman	George Bowman	. . . .
. . . .	Samuel Baldwin	Samuel Baldwin	. . . .
. . . .	Benjamin Blackburn	Benjamin Blackburn	. . . .
. . . .	John Becket	John Becket	. . . .
. . . .	John Baylis	. . . .	. . . .
. . . .	Charles Buck	Charles Buck	. . . .
. . . .	. . . .	Josiah Ballenger	Josiah Ballenger
. . . .	. . . .	Robert Buckles	Robert Buckles
Col. John Carlyle	Col. John Carlyle	. . . .	. . . .
Dr. James Craik	Dr. James Craik	. . . .	. . . .
William Cockran	William Cockran	. . . .	. . . .
Andrew Calvin	. . . .	Andrew Calvin	. . . .
Martin Cryler	Martin Cryler	. . . .	. . . .
Simon Carson	Simon Carson	. . . .	. . . .
Christopher Clark	Christopher Clark	. . . .	. . . .
David Chester	David Chester	. . . .	. . . .
Jacob Cockener	Jacob Cockener	. . . .	. . . .
Thomas Chester	Thomas Chester	. . . .	. . . .
John Cook	John Cook	. . . .	. . . .
Henry Clud	Henry Cloud	. . . .	. . . .
Nathaniel Carr	Nathaniel Carr	. . . .	. . . .
Matthew Calman	Matthew Calman	. . . .	. . . .
Edward Corder	Edward Corder	. . . .	. . . .
William Cromley	. . . .	William Cromley	. . . .
Robert Cunningham	. . . .	Robert Cunningham	. . . .
John Cromley	. . . .	John Cromley	. . . .
Joshua Calvin	. . . .	Joshua Calvin	. . . .
Jacob Cowper	Jacob Cowper	. . . .	. . . .
Thomas Carner	. . . .	Thomas Carney	. . . .
William Cocks	William Cocks	. . . .	. . . .
Valentine Crawford	. . . .	Valentine Crawford	. . . .
Junior	. . . .	Junior	. . . .
John Colston	. . . .	John Colston	. . . .
Thomas Cooper	Thomas Cooper	. . . .	. . . .
John Chenoweth	. . . .	John Chenoweth	. . . .
William Coil	. . . .	William Coil	. . . .
James Carter Jr.	. . . .	James Carter Jr.	. . . .
Edward Cartmell	Edward Cartmell	. . . .	. . . .
Joseph Combs	Joseph Combs	. . . .	. . . .
William Chambers	William Chambers	. . . .	. . . .
. . . .	James Carter	James Carter	. . . .
. . . .	William Chaplin	William Chaplin	. . . .
. . . .	Thomas Caton	Thomas Caton	. . . .
. . . .	Thomas Colston	Thomas Colston	. . . .
. . . .	James Cromley	James Cromley	. . . .
. . . .	William Calmes	William Calmes	. . . .
. . . .	. . . .	Thomas Cordery	Thomas Cordery
Charles Dick	Charles Dick	. . . .	. . . .

51

Washington	Martin	West	Swearingen
John Dyer	John Dyer	. . . .	. . . .
Edward Dodd	. . . .	Edward Dodd	. . . .
David Dedrick	David Dedrick	. . . .	. . . .
Thomas Doster	. . . .	Thomas Doster	. . . .
John Dow	John Dow	. . . .	. . . .
Patrick Duncan	Patrick Duncan	. . . .	. . . .
. . . .	William Duckworth	William Duckworth	. . . .
Isaac Evans	. . . .	. . . .	Isaac Evans
William Evans	William Evans	. . . .	. . . .
Josiah Edwards Jr.	Josiah Edwards Jr.	. . . .	. . . .
William Ewings	William Ewings	. . . .	. . . .
. . . .	Henry Easton	Henry Easton	. . . .
. . . .	Thomas Ellis	Thomas Ellis	. . . .
Thomas Lord Fairfax	Thomas Lord Fairfax	. . . .	. . . .
Paul Frowman	Paul Frowman	. . . .	. . . .
Richard Foley	Richard Foley	. . . .	. . . .
Abraham Fry	Abraham Fry	. . . .	. . . .
Jacob Fry	Jacob Fry	. . . .	. . . .
Joseph Fry	Joseph Fry	. . . .	. . . .
Benjamin Fry	Benjamin Fry	. . . .	. . . .
Henry Funk	Henry Funk	. . . .	. . . .
Martin Funk	Martin Funk	. . . .	. . . .
Joseph Fossett (Fawcett)	Joseph Fossett (Fawcett)	. . . .	. . . .
Samuel Fry	Samuel Fry	. . . .	. . . .
Joseph Funk	Joseph Funk	. . . .	. . . .
John Funkhouser	John Funkhouser	. . . .	. . . .
Richard Fosset (Fawcett)	Richard Fosset (Fawcett)	. . . .	. . . .
William Frost	. . . .	William Frost	. . . .
Matthias Funk	Matthias Funk	. . . .	. . . .
George Farrar	George Farrar	. . . .	. . . .
Isaac Foster	. . . .	Isaac Foster	. . . .
Col. Geo. W. Fairfax	Col. Geo. W. Fairfax	. . . .	. . . .
John Fosset (Fawcett)	John Fosset (Fawcett)	. . . .	. . . .
Capt. John Funk	Capt. John Funk	. . . .	. . . .
. . . .	John Fife	John Fife	. . . .
. . . .	Martin Funk	Martin Funk	. . . .
John Glenn	. . . .	. . . .	John Glenn
David Glass	David Glass	. . . .	. . . .
James Grinnan	James Grinnan	. . . .	. . . .
William Glover	William Glover	. . . .	. . . .
William Gaddis	. . . .	William Gaddis	. . . .
Joseph Glass	Joseph Glass	. . . .	. . . .
Robert Glass	. . . .	Robert Glass	. . . .
John Grinnan	John Grinnan	. . . .	. . . .
Christopher Grable	Christopher Grable	. . . .	. . . .
Philip Glass	Philip Glass	. . . .	. . . .
. . . .	Edward Griffith	Edward Griffith	. . . .
. . . .	Jacob Gibson	Jacob Gibson	. . . .
Adam Hunter	Adam Hunter	. . . .	. . . .
Noah Hampton	Noah Hampton	. . . .	. . . .
John Harbinger	John Harbinger	. . . .	. . . .

Washington	Martin	West	Swearingen
Rev. John Hoge	Rev. John Hoge	. . . .	. . . .
George Hardin	George Hardin	. . . .	. . . .
John Housman	John Housman	. . . .	. . . .
James Hoge Jr.	. . . .	James Hoge Jr.	. . . .
Henry Heth	. . . .	Henry Heth	. . . .
George Henry	George Henry	. . . .	. . . .
Nicholas Hanshaw	. . . .	Nicholas Hanshaw	. . . .
Thomas Hart	. . . .	Thomas Hart	. . . .
Robert Harper	. . . .	Robert Harper	. . . .
George Huddle	George Huddle	. . . .	. . . .
Murtle Handley	. . . .	Murtle Handley	. . . .
John Harrom	. . . .	John Harrom	. . . .
John Hope	John Hope	. . . .	. . . .
Jacob Hite	. . . .	Jacob Hite	. . . .
. . . .	Stephen Hotzenbell	Stephen Hotzenbell	. . . .
. . . .	Robert Halpenny	. . . .	Robert Halpenny
. . . .	Godgrey Humbert	Godfrey Humbert	. . . .
. . . .	Thomas Hampton	Thomas Hampton	. . . .
. . . .	Robert Haines	. . . .	Robert Haines
Col. John Hite	Col. John Hite	. . . .	. . . .
. . . .	James Hog	James Hog	. . . .
. . . .	Thomas Helms	Thomas Helms	. . . .
. . . .	William Helms	William Helms	. . . .
. . . .	Richard Highland	Richard Highland	. . . .
. . . .	. . . .	George Hampton	George Hampton
. . . .	. . . .	Simeon Hyat	Simeon Hyat
. . . .	. . . .	Joseph Harner	Joseph Harner
. . . .	. . . .	James Hedge	James Hedge
. . . .	. . . .	John House	John House
Isaac Hite	. . . .	. . . .	. . . .
Peter Jordan	Peter Jordan	. . . .	. . . .
Aaron Jenkins	. . . .	. . . .	Aaron Jenkins
Daniel Johnston	. . . .	Daniel Johnston	. . . .
Robert Johnston Gent	Robert Johnston Gent	. . . .	. . . .
Stephen Johnston	. . . .	Stephen Johnston	. . . .
Joshua Jones	. . . .	Joshua Jones	. . . .
John Jones	. . . .	John Jones	. . . .
William Jolliffe Jr.	. . . .	William Jolliffe Jr.	. . . .
Gabriel Jones Gent	Gabriel Jones Gent	. . . .	. . . .
. . . .	. . . .	Samuel Isaacs	. . . .
George Keller	George Keller	. . . .	. . . .
James Knight	James Knight	. . . .	. . . .
. . . .	. . . .	John Keywood	John Keywood
Lewis Fields Esq.	Lewis Fields Esq.	. . . .	. . . .
Thomas Lemon	Thomas Lemon	. . . .	. . . .
Joseph Lupton	. . . .	Joseph Lupton	. . . .
William Lupton	. . . .	William Lupton	. . . .
Edward Lucas	. . . .	. . . .	Edward Lucas
Samuel Littler	. . . .	Samuel Littler	. . . .
James Lloyd	. . . .	James Lloyd	. . . .
Andrew Longacre	Andrew Longacre	. . . .	. . . .
Joshua Langdon	Joshua Langdon	. . . .	. . . .
Geo. Michael Lorenger	. . . .	Geo. Michael Lorenger	. . . .

Washington	Martin	West	Swearingen
Francis Lilburn	. . . .	Fancis Lilburn	. . . .
George Lochmiller	George Lochmiller	. . . .	. . . .
Isaac Laren	Isaac Laren	. . . .	. . . .
Robert Lemon	. . . .	Robert Lemon	. . . .
. . . .	John Lemon	John Lemon	. . . .
. . . .	John Leith	John Leigh	. . . .
. . . .	Nicholas Lemon	Nicholas Lemon	. . . .
. . . .	Henry Loyd	Henry Loyd	. . . .
. . . .	John Lindsay	John Lindsay	. . . .
. . . .	. . . .	James Lindsay	James Lindsay
. . . .	. . . .	Thomas Loudon	Thomas Loudon
. . . .	. . . .	Edmonds Lindsay	Edmond Lindsay
Rev. William Meldrum	Rev. William Meldrum	. . . .	. . . .
William McGee	. . . .	. . . .	William McGee
David Miller	. . . .	. . . .	David Miller
Robert Marney	Robert Marney	. . . .	. . . .
John McDowell	John McDowell	. . . .	. . . .
David Morgan	. . . .	David Morgan	. . . .
William McMahan	. . . .	William McMahan	. . . .
Richard McMahan	. . . .	Richard McMahan	. . . .
John Milburn	. . . .	. . . .	John Milburn
James McGill	. . . .	James McGill	. . . .
Robert McCoy	Robert McCoy	. . . .	. . . .
Laughlin Madden	. . . .	Laughlin Madden	. . . .
Joseph McCormick	. . . .	Joseph McCormick	. . . .
John Maddin	John Maddin	. . . .	. . . .
John McCormick	John McCormick	. . . .	. . . .
Joseph McCormick	. . . .	Joseph McCormick	. . . .
Henry Moore Gent	Henry Moore Gent	. . . .	. . . .
Robert Milburn	. . . .	Robert Milburn	. . . .
Darby McCarty	Darby McCarty	. . . .	. . . .
William Monger	. . . .	William Monger	. . . .
William Miller	William Miller	. . . .	. . . .
Thomas Mason	. . . .	Thomas Mason	. . . .
Darby Murphy	Darby Murphy	. . . .	. . . .
Patrick McDaniel	Patrick McDaniel	. . . .	. . . .
Lewis Moore	Lewis Moore	. . . .	. . . .
. . . .	Richard Mercer	Richard Mercer	. . . .
. . . .	Mayberry Maddin	Mayberry Maddin	. . . .
. . . .	Col. M. Morgan	Col. M. Morgan	. . . .
. . . .	Richard Morgan	Richard Morgan	. . . .
. . . .	Jacob Miller	Jacob Miller	. . . .
. . . .	Edward Mercer Jr.	Edward Mercer Jr.	. . . .
. . . .	. . . .	John Mendenhall	John Mendenhall
. . . .	. . . .	Morgan Morgan Jr.	Morgan Morgan Jr.
. . . .	. . . .	Jacob Moon	Jacob Moon
George Neirl	George Neirl	. . . .	. . . .
. . . .	John Nisewanger	John Nisewanger	. . . .
Isaac Parkins	. . . .	Isaac Parkins	. . . .
Nicholas Princeller	Nicholas Princeller	. . . .	. . . .
Michael Poker	Michael Poker	. . . .	. . . .
William Patterson	. . . .	. . . .	William Patterson
George Paul	. . . .	. . . .	George Paul
Charles Perkins	. . . .	Charles Perkins	. . . .
Lawrence Pence	Lawrence Pence	. . . .	. . . .

Washington	Martin	West	Swearingen
William Peckering	. . . .	William Peckering	. . . .
. . . .	. . . .	Samuel Pearson	Samuel Pearson
. . . .	. . . .	Job Pugh	Job Pugh
Jesse Pugh	. . . .	Jesse Pugh	. . . .
Thomas Postgate	Thomas Postgate	. . . .	. . . .
Josiah Pemberton	. . . .	Josiah Pemberton	. . . .
Joseph Parrell	. . . .	Joseph Parrell	. . . .
John Parrell	. . . .	John Parrell	. . . .
Peter Perry	Peter Perry	. . . .	. . . .
Philip Poker	Philip Poker	. . . .	. . . .
Thomas Perry	Thomas Perry	. . . .	. . . .
Azariah Pugh	. . . .	Azariah Pugh	. . . .
Jonathan Perkins	. . . .	Jonathan Perkins	. . . .
. . . .	John Painter	. . . .	John Painter
. . . .	Robert Pearis	Robert Pearis	. . . .
. . . .	Thomas Pugh	Thomas Pugh	. . . .
. . . .	Samuel Pritchard	Samuel Pritchard	. . . .
. . . .	. . . .	George Pemberton	George Pemberton
William Russell	William Russell	. . . .	. . . .
John Road	John Road	. . . .	. . . .
Robert Rutherford	Robert Rutherford	. . . .	. . . .
Thomas Reece	. . . .	Thomas Reece	. . . .
Jacob Reece	. . . .	Jacob Reece	. . . .
Henry Rinker	. . . .	Henry Rinker	. . . .
George Ross	. . . .	George Ross	. . . .
Patick Rice	. . . .	Patrick Rice	. . . .
George Rice	. . . .	George Rice	. . . .
William Reynolds	. . . .	William Reynolds	. . . .
Isaac Riddell	Isaac Riddell	. . . .	. . . .
Henry Reece	. . . .	Henry Reece	. . . .
William Roberts	William Roberts	. . . .	. . . .
William Roberts Jr.	William Roberts Jr.	. . . .	. . . .
John Reed	. . . .	. . . .	. . . .
Ulrich Rubble	. . . .	Ulrich Rubble	. . . .
. . . .	Joseph Roberts	Joseph Roberts	. . . .
. . . .	Edward Rogers	Edward Rogers	. . . .
Cornel Ruddle	Cornel Ruddell	. . . .	. . . .
Lt. Charles Smith	. . . .	Lt. Charles Smith	. . . .
John Smith	John Smith	. . . .	. . . .
Peter Stephens	Peter Stephens	. . . .	. . . .
John Snap	John Snap	. . . .	. . . .
John Snap Jr.	John Snap Jr.	. . . .	. . . .
Daniel Stover	Daniel Stover	. . . .	. . . .
Henry Stephens	Henry Stephens	. . . .	. . . .
Jacob Strickler	Jacob Strickler	. . . .	. . . .
Benjamin Strickler	Benjamin Strickler	. . . .	. . . .
David Snodgrass	. . . .	. . . .	David Snodgrass
Lawrence Smallgolfer	Lawrence Smallgolfer	. . . .	. . . .
Nicholas Schrack	. . . .	Nicholas Schrack	. . . .
Ulrich Stoner	Ulrich Stoner	. . . .	. . . .
Robert Stewart	. . . .	Robert Stewart	. . . .
Jacob Sowers	. . . .	Jacob Sowers	. . . .
Jonas Seaman	. . . .	. . . .	Jonas Seaman
John Stickley	John Stickley	. . . .	. . . .

55

Washington	Martin	West	Swearingen
John Sewell	. . . .	. . . .	John Sewell
Jacob Sebert	. . . .	Jacob Sebert	. . . .
Joseph Stickler	Joseph Strickler	. . . .	. . . .
Thomas Shepherd	. . . .	Thomas Shepherd	. . . .
David Shepherd	. . . .	David Shepherd	. . . .
John Small	. . . .	John Small	. . . .
Lewis Stephens	Lewis Stephens	. . . .	. . . .
Jacob Stover	Jacob Stover	. . . .	. . . .
Dennis Springer	. . . .	Dennis Springer	. . . .
Richard Stephenson	Richard Stephenson	. . . .	. . . .
Edward Snickers	Edward Snickers	. . . .	. . . .
Lawrence Snapp	Lawrence Snapp	. . . .	. . . .
Robert Stewart	. . . .	Robert Stewart	. . . .
Daniel Stephens	. . . .	Daniel Stephens	. . . .
George Shade	George Shade	. . . .	. . . .
Thomas Speake	. . . .	Thomas Speake	. . . .
. . . .	Lawrence Stephens	Lawrence Stephens	. . . .
. . . .	Thomas Sharp	Thomas Sharp	. . . .
. . . .	Jeremiah Smith	Jeremiah Smith	. . . .
. . . .	Peter Stover	Peter Stover	. . . .
. . . .	William Stephenson	William Stephenson	. . . .
. . . .	John Scene	John Scene	. . . .
		John Stroud	John Stroud
Joseph Thompson	. . . .	Joseph Thompson	. . . .
Evan Thomas	. . . .	Evan Thomas	. . . .
John Thomas	John Thomas	. . . .	. . . .
Samuel Taylor	. . . .	Samuel Taylor	. . . .
Anthony Turner	. . . .	Anthony Turner	. . . .
Ellis Thomas	Ellis Thomas	. . . .	. . . .
Anthony Turner Jr.	. . . .	Anthony Turner Jr.	. . . .
Harrison Taylor	Harrison Taylor	. . . .	. . . .
Edward Thomas	. . . .	Edward Thomas	. . . .
. . . .	Zebulon Sharp	Zebulon Sharp	. . . .
. . . .	Simon Taylor	Simon Taylor	. . . .
. . . .	. . . .	Owen Thomas	Owen Thomas
. . . .	. . . .	John Taylor	John Taylor
. . . .	. . . .	Magnus Tate	Magnus Tate
Alexander Vance	. . . .	. . . .	Alexander Vance
James Vance	James Vance	. . . .	. . . .
Samuel Vance	Samuel Vance	. . . .	. . . .
Andrew Vance	Andrew Vance	. . . .	. . . .
John Vanmeter	. . . .	. . . .	John Vanmeter
Abram Vanmeter	. . . .	. . . .	Abram Vanmeter
John Vestal	. . . .	. . . .	John Vestal
Jacob Vanmeter	. . . .	Jacob Vanmeter	. . . .
John Vance	John Vance	. . . .	. . . .
Henry Vanmeter	. . . .	Henry Vanmeter	. . . .
John Frederick Vanfagan	John Frederick Vanfagan	. . . .	. . . .
. . . .	David Vance	David Vance	. . . .
. . . .	Joseph Vance	Joseph Vance	. . . .
. . . .	William Vance	William Vance	. . . .
Col. James Wood	. . . .	Col. James Wood	. . . .
Alexander Woodrow Gent	. . . .		. . . .

George Washington's Headquarters
1899

Washington	Martin	West	Swearingen
Peter Woolf	Peter Woolf	. . . .	. . . .
Isaac White	Isaac White	. . . .	. . . .
George Whitzel	George Whitzel	. . . .	. . . .
James Wright	. . . .	James Wright	. . . .
Robert Wilson	Robert Wilson	. . . .	. . . .
George Wright	George Wright	. . . .	. . . .
Jacob Wright	Jacob Wright	. . . .	. . . .
David Wright	David Wright	. . . .	. . . .
Christian Wendall	Christian Wendall	. . . .	. . . .
August Wendall	August Wendall	. . . .	. . . .
James Wilson	James Wilson	. . . .	. . . .
Valentine Wendall	Valentine Wendall	. . . .	. . . .
Thomas Waters	Thomas Waters	. . . .	. . . .
Joseph Wilkinson	. . . .	Joseph Wilkinson	. . . .
Robert Worthington	. . . .	Robert Worthington	. . . .
Ralph Withers	Ralph Withers	. . . .	. . . .
John Wilson	. . . .	John Wilson	. . . .
John Wright	John Wright	. . . .	. . . .
William White	. . . .	William White	
. . . .	William Wilson	. . . .	William Wilson
. . . .	Robert Warth	Robert Warth	. . . .
John Young	John Young	. . . .	. . . .

Result of Poll for Burgesses from Frederick County
Held in Winchester May 18, 1761

(From Washington Manuscript, Library of Congress)

Col. George Washington	Col. George Mercer	Col. Adam Stephen
John Washington	John Washington	. . . .
Samuel Washington	Samuel Washington	. . . .
George Ross	George Ross	. . . .
. . . .	Lewis W. Moore (?)	Lewis W. Moore (?)
Isaac Hite	Isaac Hite	. . . .
James Mercer	James Mercer	. . . .
James Wood	James Wood	. . . .
Fielding Lewis	Fielding Lewis	. . . .
Jonah Hedge	Jonah Hedge	. . . .
Benjamin Rutherford	. . . .	Benjamin Rutherford
John Pierce	John Pierce	. . . .
Peter Fletcher	Peter Fletcher	. . . .
William Davis	. . . .	William Davis
Richard Fletcher	Rrchard Fletcher	. . . .
Robert Wilson	. . . .	Robert Wilson
John Snap	John Snap	. . . .
John Hope	John Hope	. . . .
John Miller	John Miller	. . . .
Philip Glass	Philip Glass	. . . .
. . . .	John Dyer	John Dyer
Thomas Swearingen	Thomas Swearingen	. . . .
Richard Hogeland	Richard Hogeland	. . . .
Magnus Tate	. . . .	Magnus Tate
. . . .	Richard Mercer	Richard Mercer
John Snap Jr.	John Snap Jr.	. . . .
. . . .	Thomas Babb Jr.	Thomas Babb Jr.
Joseph Boshier	. . . .	Joseph Boshier
Jacob Miller	Jacob Miller	. . . .
Henry Moyer	Henry Moyer	. . . .
Thomas Pugh	Thomas Pugh	. . . .
Mayberry Maddin	Mayberry Maddin	. . . .
James Craik	James Craik	. . . .
Earnest Ender	Earnest Ender	. . . .
George Maurer	George Maurer	. . . .
Edward Davis	Edward Davis	. . . .
Barnard Syler	Barnard Syler	. . . .
Charles Washington	Charles Washington	. . . .
Thomas Branson	. . . .	Thomas Branson
Nicholas Baker	Nicholas Baker	. . . .
David Vance	. . . .	David Vance
John Vanmeter	. . . .	John Vanmeter
James Stroud	. . . .	James Stroud
. . . .	James Morris	James Morris
Lewis Pearce	Lewis Pearce	. . . .
Edward Beason	. . . .	Edward Beason

Washington	Mercer	Stephen
....	Murtry Handley	Murtry Handley
Thomas Wilson	....	Thomas Wilson
James Hoge	James Hoge	....
....	William Evans	William Evans
Abram Vanmetre	Abram Vametre	....
Jacob Strickler	....	Jacob Strickler
Joseph Strickler	....	Joseph Strickler
John Rhodes	....	John Rhodes
Edward Wilson	....	Edward Wilson
Jacob Burner	....	Jacob Burner
Anthony Turner	Anthony Turner	....
Taliaferro Stribling	Taliaferro Stribling	....
David Miller	....	David Miller
John Strickler	John Stickler	....
....	James Brown	James Brown
Peter Stover	Peter Stover	....
Lewis Pence	Lewis Pence	....
John Tipton	John Tipton	....
....	Enos Thomas	Enos Thomas
Robert Lucas	....	Robert Lucas
William White	....	William White
Jacob Fry	Jacob Fry	....
....	William McMachen	William McMachen
Conrad Oranamus	....	Conrad Oranamus
Jacob Moon	Jacob Moon	....
....	John Thomas	John Thomas
Samuel Brown	....	Samuel Brown
....	Douglas Campbell	Douglas Campbell
James Davis	James Davis	....
William Russle (Russel)	....	William Russle (Russel)
John Snodgrass	....	John Snodgrass
....	William Foster	William Foster
John Feawood (?)	....	....
Edward Lucas	....	Edward Lucas
John Jenkins	John Jenkins	....
Henry Moore	Henry Moore	....
Lewis Pearce	Lewis Pearce	....
William White Jr.	....	William White Jr.
Hugh Rankins	....	Hugh Rankins
Lunis Hood	Lunis Hood	....
Benjamin Barrat (Barrett)	Benjamin Barrat (Barrett)	....
Owen Roberts	Owne Roberts	....
William Russell	....	William Russell
Burr Harrison	....	Burr Harrison
Joseph Langdon	....	Joseph Langdon
Thomas Rutherford	Thomas Rugherford	....
George Hoge Jr.	George Hoge Jr.	....
William Hobson	William Hobson	....
Joseph White	....	Joseph White
John Fife	John Fife	....
Jonathan Langdon	....	Jonathan Langdon
Michael Wolfe	Michael Wolfe	....
Benjamin Fry	Benjamin Fry	....
Samuel Fry	Samuel Fry	....
George Deviney (?)	George Deviney (?)	....

Washington	Mercer	Stephen
Reuben Moore	. . . .	Reuben Moore
Jacob Woolf	Jacob Woolf	. . . .
George Pemberton	. . . .	George Pemberton
James Loyd	. . . .	James Loyd
Ulrich Keaner	Ulrich Keaner	. . . .
Jeremiah Strode	. . . .	Jermiah Strode
Joseph Harner	Joseph Harner	. . . .
John Littler	John Littler	. . . .
Jacob Sterly	Jacob Sterly	. . . .
Edward Robinson	Edward Robinson	. . . .
Jacob Beller	. . . .	Jacob Beller
James Magill	James Magill	. . . .
Isaac Larew	. . . .	Isaac Larew
. . . .	Moses Lambert	. . . .
. . . .	Morgan Morgan	Morgan Morgan
Elisha Isaacs	Elisha Isaacs	. . . .
. . . .	Isaac Brown	Isaac Brown
Josiah Ballinger	Josiah Ballinger	. . . .
. . . .	Tobias Burk	Tobias Burk
Richard Stephenson	. . . .	Richard Stephenson
David Glass	David Glass	. . . .
William Merchant	William Merchant	. . . .
James Wilson	. . . .	James Wilson
Jacob Wright	. . . .	Jacob Wright
Hugh Haines	Hugh Haines	. . . .
. . . .	John McMachen	John McMachen
Joseph McDowel	. . . .	Joseph McDowel
Joseph Edwards Jr.	. . . .	Joseph Edwards Jr.
Edward Thomas	. . . .	Edward Thomas
George McKenney	. . . .	George McKenney
Thomas Hampton	Thomas Hampton	. . . .
Leonard Baldwin	Leonard Baldwin	. . . .
Michael Poker	Michael Poker	. . . .
. . . .	William Stewart	William Stewart
Peter Hanger	Peter Hanger	. . . .
. . . .	Evan Thomas	Evan Thomas
Jacob Christman	Jacob Christman	. . . .
John Smith	. . . .	John Smith
William Philips	. . . .	William Philips
Joseph Thompson	Joseph Thompson	. . . .
Thomas Berry	Thomas Berry	. . . .
David Osbourne	. . . .	David Osbourne
William Rankin	. . . .	William Rankin
John Abril	. . . .	John Abril
David Rankin	. . . .	David Rankin
Charles Littleton	Charles Littleton	. . . .
William Hogg	William Hogg	. . . .
John Colson	John Colson	. . . .
Joseph Hill	Joseph Hill	. . . .
. . . .	Matthias Grove	Matthias Grove
Alexander Ogleby	Alexander Ogleby	. . . .
Walter Shirley	. . . .	Walter Shirley
Jacob Miller the Elder	Jacob Miller the Elder	. . . .
. . . .	Frederick Pleubert	Frederick Pleubert
George Hampton	George Hampton	. . . .

Washington	Mercer	Stephen
George Bruce	. . . .	George Bruce
Anthony Pitman	Anthony Pitman	. . . .
Thomas Allan	. . . .	Thomas Allan
Frederick Shiebly	. . . .	Frederick Shiebly
John Taylor	John Taylor	. . . .
James Barber	James Barber	. . . .
Henry Baker	Henry Baker	. . . .
Owen Winkfield	Owen Winkfield	. . . .
George Shoemaker	George Shoemaker	. . . .
. . . .	Andrew Colvin	Andrew Colvin
William Clark	William Clark	. . . .
Thomas Chester	. . . .	Thomas Chester
William Rogers	William Rogers	. . . .
Samuel Ackline	Samuel Ackline	. . . .
. . . .	Edward Griffith	Edward Griffith
Christopher Hockman	Christopher Hockman	. . . .
James Glann (Glen)	. . . .	James Glann (Glen)
. . . .	George Bowman	George Bowman
Richard Fosset (Fawcett)	Richard Fosset (Fawcett)	. . . .
John Glann (Glen)	. . . .	John Glann (Glen)
Abarham Daste (?)	Abraham Daste (?)	. . . .
Jacob Cocknover	Jacob Cocknover	. . . .
(Gochenour)	(Gochenour)	. . . .
John Parke	. . . .	John Parke
John Fonkhouser	John Fonkhouser	. . . .
(Funkhouser)	(Funkhouser)	. . . .
Henry Frables	Henry Frables	. . . .
. . . .	Daniel Shibley	Daniel Shibley
George Seller	George Seller	. . . .
Samuel Newal	. . . .	Samuel Newal
John Pennywit (?)	John Pennywit (?)	. . . .
John Snodgrass	. . . .	John Snodgrass
John Plank	John Plank	. . . .
Robert Bull	. . . .	Robert Bull
Thomas Perry	Thomas Perry	. . . .
Abraham Fry	Abraham Fry	. . . .
. . . .	John Funk	John Funk
Samuel Bailey	Samuel Bailey	. . . .
. . . .	Joseph Funk	Joseph Funk
Isaac Evans	. . . .	Isaac Evans
John Grable	John Grable	. . . .
Jacob Bowman	Jacob Bowman	. . . .
John Lupton	. . . .	John Lupton
Samuel Sawyer (?)	Samuel Sawyer (?)	. . . .
Isaac Mellan (?)	Isaac Mellan (?)	. . . .
Thomas Bryan Martin	. . . .	Thomas Bryan Martin
Peter Ruble	Peter Ruble	. . . .
Thomas Wright	Thomas Wright	. . . .
. . . .	Martin Rowler	Martin Rowler
Rev. John Hoge	. . . .	Rev. John Hoge
Edmund Rice	Edmund Rice	. . . .
David Ruble	David Ruble	. . . .
Richard Pearis	. . . .	Richard Pearis
Edward Dodd	. . . .	Edward Dodd
Darby McCarty	. . . .	Darby McCarty

Washington	Mercer	Stephen
Charles Brounfield	Charles Brounfield	. . . .
. . . .	Stephen Hart	Stephen Hart
. . . .	John Watson	John Watson
Sichman Handley	Sichman Handley	. . . .
George Keller	. . . .	George Keller
Job Pugh	Job Pugh	. . . .
Van Swaringen	Van Swaringen	. . . .
Lawrence Linder	Lawrence Linder	. . . .
Thomas Lowe	Thomas Lowe	. . . .
. . . .	John Shearer	John Shearer
Joseph Babb	Joseph Babb	. . . .
. . . .	Philip Elphenston (Helphenstine)	Philip Elphenston (Helphenstine)
. . . .	Simon Carson	Simon Carson
George Follis	George Follis	. . . .
John Hite	John Hite	. . . .
. . . .	Alexander Ross	Alexander Ross
Jacob Bowman the Elder	Jacob Bowman the Elder	. . . .
George Ogle (?)	George Ogle (?)	. . . .
. . . .	David Lewis	David Lewis
John Parrel	John Parrel	. . . .
Jacob Fonkhouser (Funkhouser)	Jacob Fonkhouser (Funkhouser)	. . . .
Reynold Baldwin	Reynold Baldwin	. . . .
Matthew Seltzer	. . . .	Matthew Seltzer
Henry Easton	Henry Easton	. . . .
Thomas Kennady	. . . .	Thomas Kennady
Peter Holler	. . . .	Peter Holler
Cornelius Ruddle	. . . .	Cornelius Ruddle
John Thomas	John Thomas	. . . .
Henry Pike	Henry Pike	. . . .
William Hiat	. . . .	William Hiat
. . . .	Henry Mercersmith	Henry Mercersmith
Andrew Longacre	Andrew Longacre	. . . .
John Chenoweth	. . . .	John Chenoweth
. . . .	Lawrence Stephens	Lawrence Stephens
George Houghacker	George Houghacker	. . . .
. . . .	Alexander McDonald	Alexander McDonald
Christian Windle	Christian Windle	. . . .
Martin Black	. . . .	Martin Black
Frederick Beeler	Frederick Beeler	. . . .
. . . .	Henry Heth	Henry Heth
. . . .	John Nealy	John Nealy
George Henry	. . . .	George Henry
John Evans	. . . .	John Evans
Reuben Paxton	. . . .	Reuben Paxton
. . . .	William Cromley Jr.	William Cromley Jr.
. . . .	Febalt (?) Passan (?)	Febalt (?) Passan (?)
Henry Conrad	. . . .	Henry Conrad
Nicholas Harwich	Nicholas Harwich	. . . .
William Ramey	William Ramey	. . . .
Henry Vanmeter	Henry Vanmeter	. . . .
George Jenkins	George Jenkins	. . . .
Walter Newman	. . . .	Walter Newman
Patrick Rice	Patrick Rice	. . . .
Jacob Vanmeter	. . . .	Jacob Vanmeter

Washington	Mercer	Stephen
Paulso (?) Fan (?)	Paulso (?) Fan (?)	. . . .
. . . .	Mercer Babb	Mercer Babb
John Wilson	. . . .	John Wilson
William McKey	. . . .	William McKey
. . . .	Henry Stephens	Henry Stephens
Jacob Vanmetre	Jacob Vanmetre	. . . .
Nicholas Piger (?)	Nicholas Piger (?)	. . . .
George Weaver	George Weaver	. . . .
Stephen Trinkle	Stephen Trinkle	. . . .
Tevalt Eagle	Tevalt Eagle	. . . .
Abraham Denton	. . . .	Abraham Denton
Samuel Sample	. . . .	Samuel Sample
William Stroupe	. . . .	William Stroupe
Jacob Giger	Jacob Giger	. . . .
John Allan	. . . .	John Allan
Valnetine Crawford	. . . .	Valentine Crawford
. . . .	Peter Woolfe (Wolf)	Peter Woolfe (Wolfe)
Robert Glass	. . . .	Robert Glass
Andrew Vance	. . . .	Andrew Vance
. . . .	Peter Stephens	Peter Stephens
Samuel Vance	. . . .	Samuel Vance
Peter Jordan	. . . .	Peter Jordan
Jackson Allan	Jackson Allan	. . . .
Nicholas McIntire	. . . .	Nicholas McIntire
James Ballenger	James Ballenger	. . . .
John Anderson	John Anderson	. . . .
Robert Wilson Junior	. . . .	Robert Wilson Junior
Owen Thomas	. . . .	Owen Thomas
Robert Wilson Sr.	Robert Wilson Sr.	. . . .
Emanuel Boges (?)	Emanuel Boges (?)	. . . .
Nicholas Handshaw	Nicholas Handshaw	. . . .
John Brown	John Brown	. . . .
Michael March	Michael March	. . . .
Lewis Stephens	. . . .	Lewis Stephens
Abraham Brubecker	. . . .	Abraham Brubecker
Benjamin Blackburn	. . . .	Benjamin Blackburn
. . . .	William Stinson	William Stinson
George Ruddle	. . . .	George Ruddle
. . . .	Samuel Blackburn	Samuel Blackburn
Samuel Vance	. . . .	Samuel Vance
George Poker	George Poker	. . . .
Zebulon Tharp	. . . .	Zebulon Tharp
Morrice Reece	. . . .	Morrice Reece
George Snider	. . . .	George Snider
Joshua Hedge	Joshua Hedge	. . . .
John Bridger	John Bridger	. . . .
Joseph Lupton	. . . .	Joseph Lupton
. . . .	James Moore	James Moore
Jarvis Daugherty	. . . .	Jarvis Daugherty
William Daugherty	. . . .	William Daugherty
. . . .	Abraham Taylor	Abraham Taylor
Robert Lemon	. . . .	Robert Lemon
William Wright	. . . .	William Wright
Benj. Thornberry	. . . .	Benj. Thornberry
George Hollingsworth	. . . .	George Hollingsworth

Washington	Mercer	Stephen
Hugh Lyle	. . . .	Hugh Lyle
Robert Worthington	. . . .	Robert Worthington
William Crawford	. . . .	William Crawford
James McCormack	. . . .	Jamces McCormack
James Knight	. . . .	James Knight
Barnard Newkirk	Barnard Newkirk	. . . .
. . . .	Jonas Seaman	Jonas Seaman
. . . .	David Allan	David Allan
William Coil	. . . .	William Coil
. . . .	Richard Calvert	Richard Calvert
Isaac Foster	Isaac Foster	. . . .
Alexander Woodrow	Alexander Woodrow	. . . .
William Patterson	. . . .	William Patterson
George Wright	. . . .	George Wright
Richard Barber	. . . .	Richard Barber
John Stroud	. . . .	John Stroud
John Briscoe	. . . .	John Briscoe
James Cromley	James Cromley	. . . .
William Calmes	William Calmes	. . . .
Marquis Calmes	Marquis Calmes	. . . .
Peter Catlet	Peter Catlet	. . . .
William Frost	William Frost	. . . .
Thomas Chenoweth	Thomas Chenoweth	. . . .
Edmund Lindsey	Edmund Lindsey	. . . .
Charles Huddle	Charles Huddle	. . . .
Archibald Ruddle	. . . .	Archibald Ruddle
Valentine Windle	Valentine Windle	. . . .
Jacob Hite	Jacob Hite	. . . .
James Catlet	James Catlet	. . . .
John Vance	. . . .	John Vance
Martin Crider	. . . .	Martin Crider
Thomas Harrison	Thomas Harrison	. . . .
David Wright	. . . .	David Wright
Edward Snickers	Edward Snickers	. . . .
Peter Shull	. . . .	Peter Shull
Samuel Newman	. . . .	Samuel Newman
Samuel Newman Jr.	. . . .	Samuel Newman Jr.
Thomas Sagey	. . . .	Thomas Sagey
. . . .	Simon Snider	Simon Snider
Jacob Holdman	Jacob Holdman	. . . .
John Corlet	. . . .	John Corlet
Thomas Blackmoore	Thomas Blackmoore	. . . .
John McCormack	. . . .	John McCormack
Joseph Glass	. . . .	Joseph Glass
. . . .	Hugh Bays (?)	Hugh Bays (?)
William Vance	. . . .	William Vance
David Snodgrass	. . . .	David Snodgrass
Andrew Blackburn	. . . .	Andrew Blackburn
James Vance	. . . .	James Vance
Anthony Turner Jr.	Anthony Turner Jr.	. . . .
Jacob Gibson	Jacob Gibson	. . . .
Isaac Wright	Isaac Wright	. . . .
Augustine Windle	Augustine Windle	. . . .
. . . .	John Cromley	John Cromley
David Watkins	David Watkins	. . . .

Washington	Mercer	Stephen
Edward Read	. . . .	Edward Read
Lewis Neill	Lewis Neill	. . . .
Dennis Bow	Dennis Bow	. . . .
. . . .	Edward Mercer	Edward Mercer
Stephen Johnston	Stephen Johnston	. . . .
William Mungar	William Mungar	. . . .
Godfrey Humbert	Godfrey Humbert	. . . .
Edward Lucas Jr.	Edward Lucas Jr.	. . . .
John Davis	John Davis	. . . .
John Moyer	John Moyer	. . . .
. . . .	John Griffith	John Griffith
. . . .	Robert Paul	Robert Paul
James Hoge Jr.	. . . .	. . . .
Peter Foreman	Peter Foreman	. . . .
Tobias Otto	Tobias Otto	. . . .
Jacob Seabert	Jacob Seabert	. . . .
William Conegers (?)	William Conegers (?)	. . . .
Daniel Smith	. . . .	Daniel Smith
Azariah Pugh	Azariah Pugh	. . . .
William Chenoweth Jr.	William Chenoweth Jr.	. . . .
. . . .	Joshua Baker	Joshua Baker
. . . .	Charles Bradford	Charles Bradford
Philip Babb Jr.	Philip Babb Jr.	. . . .
William Chenoweth	William Chenoweth	. . . .
. . . .	William Gaddes	William Gaddes
James Jolliffe	James Jolliffe	. . . .
Charles Barns	. . . .	Charles Barns
. . . .	Samuel Vance	Samuel Vance
Joseph Dark	Joseph Dark	. . . .
Andrew Swan	Andrew Swan	. . . .
William Kirfert	William Kerfert	. . . .
Thomas Taylor	. . . .	Thomas Taylor
John Stonebridge	John Stonebridge	. . . .
Peter Babb	Peter Babb	. . . .
Isaac White	. . . .	Isaac White
John Prince	. . . .	John Prince
David Brooks	. . . .	David Brooks
Jacob Argenbright	Jacob Argenbright	. . . .
Robert Hodgson	. . . .	Robert Hodgson
John Becket	. . . .	John Becket
. . . .	Lawrence Hoff	Lawrence Hoff
. . . .	Moses Stricker	Moses Stricker
Robert Halfpenny	. . . .	Robert Halfpenny
George Reapsoner (?)	George Reapsoner (?)	. . . .
Henry Loyd	. . . .	Henry Loyd
. . . .	Thomas Martin	Thomas Martin
Alexander Flemon	Alexander Flemon	. . . .
Robert Harper	Robert Harper	. . . .
James Findley	. . . .	James Findley
Samuel Worthington	. . . .	Samuel Worthington
Frederick Grant	Frederick Grant	. . . .
James Colvil	James Colvil	. . . .
John Humphrey (D)	John Humphrey (D)	. . . .
William Hall	William Hall	. . . .
Robert Haines	Robert Haines	. . . .

Washington	Mercer	Stephen
Paul Froman	Paul Froman	. . . .
Archibald McNeal	. . . .	Archibald McNeal
Isiah Pemberton	Isiah Pemberton	. . . .
Jacob Reece	. . . .	Jacob Reece
Evan Rogers	Evan Rogers	. . . .
James Barnet	James Barnet	. . . .
Mathew Dunkin	. . . .	Mathew Dunkin
James Bole	. . . .	James Bole
. . . .	John Greenfield	John Greenfield
William Long	. . . .	William Long
Burkhart Reagart	Burkhart Reagart	. . . .
Tinis Neiskirk	Tunis Neiskirk	. . . .
John Branson	John Branson	. . . .
Robert Marney	Robert Marney	. . . .
Thomas Grogan	. . . .	Thomas Grogan
. . . .	William Roberts	William Roberts
John Armstrong	John Armstrong	. . . .
Edward Cartmell	Edward Cartmell	. . . .
Thomas Shephard	. . . .	Thomas Shephard
William Lupton	. . . .	William Lupton
Robert Cunningham	. . . .	Robert Cunningham
Thomas Doster	Thomas Doster	. . . .
. . . .	James Holladay	James Holladay
Simon Taylor	Simon Taylor	. . . .
. . . .	Francis Lilburn	Francis Lilburn
William Dillon	William Dillon	. . . .
Gershom Keys	Gershom Keys	. . . .
. . . .	William Raynolds	William Reynolds
Leonard Hornsby	Leonard Hornsby	. . . .
Josiah Hultz	Josiah Hultz	. . . .
Matthias Funk	Matthias Funk	. . . .
Daniel Holdman	Daniel Holdman	. . . .
John Hogeland	John Hogeland	. . . .
. . . .	Moses Mercer	Moses Mercer
William Alford	. . . .	William Alford
George Bell	George Bell	. . . .
John Reid	John Reid	. . . .
Thomas Eaton	Thomas Eaton	. . . .
Robert Sturart	Robert Stuart	. . . .
John Larrak (Larrick)	John Larrack (Larrick)	. . . .
Joseph Colvin	Joseph Colvin	. . . .
James Bruce	. . . .	James Bruce
Martin Funk	. . . .	Martin Funk
Henry Brock	Henry Brock	. . . .
William Cochran	. . . .	William Cochran
Robert McCoy	Robert McCoy	. . . .
Thomas Sharp	Thomas Sharp	. . . .
John Bordon	. . . .	John Bordon
George Nicholas	. . . .	George Nicholas
Robert White	. . . .	Robert White
William Chambers	. . . .	William Chambers
Moses Walton	. . . .	Moses Walton
George Miles	. . . .	George Miles
. . . .	Joseph Beeler	Joseph Beeler
William Glenn	. . . .	William Glenn

Washington	Mercer	Stephen
John Lemon	. . . .	John Lemon
George Ruble	George Ruble	. . . .
William Baldwin	William Baldwin	. . . .
. . . .	Thomas Csrter	Thomas Carter
Jarvis Shirley	. . . .	Jarvis Shirley
Harison Taylor	. . . .	Harison Taylor
Thomas Reece Jr.	. . . .	Thomas Reece Jr.
John Painter	. . . .	John Painter
Thomas Reece	. . . .	Thomas Reece
. . . .	William Ewing	William Ewing
. . . .	William Jones	William Jones
John Wilson	. . . .	John Wilson
. . . .	Richard McMachen	Richard McMachen
John Denton Capt.	. . . .	John Denton Capt.
Henry Bowen	Henry Bowen	. . . .
. . . .	Thomas Butler	Thomas Butler
John Housman	John Housman	. . . .
Michael Murphey	Michael Murphey	. . . .
Philip Babb	Philip Babb	. . . .
. . . .	Nathaniel Carr	Nathaniel Carr
. . . .	Joseph Reynolds	Joseph Reynolds
Robert Steward	Robert Steward	. . . .
. . . .	Everhart Daring	. . . .
. . . .	Darby Murphy	Darby Murphy
Samuel Beam	Samuel Beam	. . . .
Jonathan Taylor	Jonathan Taylor	. . . .
Lawrence Smalsapper	Lawrence Smalsapper	. . . .
Samuel Glass	Samuel Class	. . . .
Richard Hiland	Richard Hiland	. . . .
John Barrat (Barrett)	John Barrat (Barrett)	. . . .
Thomas Lindsey	Thomas Lindsey	. . . .
Charles Parkins	Charles Parkins	. . . .
Nathaniel Cartmell	Nathaniel Cartmell	. . . .
Leonard Cooper	. . . .	Leonard Cooper
William Pickering	William Pickering	. . . .
Peter Speary (Sperry)	Peter Speary (Sperry–	. . . .
Henry Knave	Henry Knave	. . . .
Moses Harling	Moses Harling	. . . .
James Barrat (Barrett)	James Barrat (Barrett)	. . . .
Thomas Ellis	Thomas Ellis	. . . .
Christian Grable	Christian Grable	. . . .
George Fetzer	George Fetzer	. . . .
George Rice	George Rice	. . . .
. . . .	Samuel Earle	Samuel Earle
John Jones	John Jones	. . . .
Josiah Springer	Josiah Springer	. . . .
John Funk Jr.	John Funk Jr.	. . . .
Henry Funk	Henry Funk	. . . .
Casper Rinker	Casper Rinker	. . . .
Jacob Sowers	. . . .	Jacob Sowers
Lawrence Snap	Lawrence Snap	. . . .
David Deadrick	. . . .	David Deadrick
Jesse Pugh	Jesse Pugh	. . . .
William Glover	. . . .	William Glover

Washington	Mercer	Stephen
. . . .	Simon Taylor	Simon Taylor
Thomas Colson	Thomas Colson	. . . .
. . . .	Charles Buck	Charles Buck
. . . .	Zachariah Morgan	Zachariah Morgan
Henry Brinker	Henry Brinker	. . . .
Robert Worth	Robert Worth	. . . .
Henry Rinker	Henry Rinker	. . . .
Frederick Conrad	Frederick Conrad	. . . .
John Mercer	John Mercer	. . . .
Charles Smith	Charles Smith	. . . .
. . . .	George Isaac Troutwine	George Isaac Troutwine
Edward Corder	. . . .	Edward Corder
George Lochmiller	. . . .	George Lochmiller
Joseph Vance	Joseph Vance	. . . .
John Hardin	. . . .	John Hardin
James Blair	. . . .	James Blair
Samuel Pearson	. . . .	Samuel Pearson
John Madden	John Madden	. . . .
Jeremiah Smith	. . . .	Jeremiah Smith
Josiah Ridgeway	. . . .	Josiah Ridgeway
Christopher Heiskel	Christopher Heiskel	. . . .
John Vestal	. . . .	John Vestal
Charles Grim	Charles Grim	. . . .
Thomas Cooper	Thomas Cooper	. . . .
James Carter	James Carter	. . . .
Stephen Hotzenbella (Hotzenbetter)	Stephen Hotzenbella (Hotzenbetter)	. . . .
. . . .	Henry Earnest	Henry Earnest
John George Dellenger	John George Dellenger	. . . .
Walter Davidson	. . . .	Walter Davidson
. . . .	David Chester	David Chester
James Grinnan	. . . .	James Grinnan
George Hotzenbella (Hotzenbetter)	George Hotzenbella (Hotzenbetter)	. . . .
Christian Lambert	Christian Lambert	. . . .
Ulrich Stoner	Ulrich Stoner	. . . .
. . . .	John Wright	John Wright
William Hawkins	William Hawkins	. . . .
Jacob Chandler	Jacob Chandler	. . . .
John Dodson	John Dodson	. . . .
. . . .	Edward Mercer Jr.	Edward Mercer Jr.
John Allison	John Allison	. . . .
Richard Foley	Richard Foley	. . . .
George Hiat	. . . .	George Hiat
Joseph Pugh	Joseph Pugh	. . . .
. . . .	Morgan Morgan Col.	Morgan Morgan Col.
. . . .	Henry Reece	Henry Reece
Owen Rogers	Owen Rogers	. . . .
Ellis Thomas	Ellis Thomas	. . . .
Robert Allan	. . . .	Robert Allan
David Morgan	. . . .	David Morgan
Jacob Kackley	Jacob Kackley	. . . .
Joseph Fosset (Fawcett)	. . . .	Joseph Fosset (Fawcett)
Thomas Carney	. . . .	Thomas Carney
Bryan Bruin	. . . .	Bryan Bruin

Washington	Mercer	Stephen
Philip Bush	Philip Bush	. . . .
Joseph Jones	Joseph Jones	. . . .
Philip Poker	Philip Poker	. . . .
. . . .	Robert Aldridge	Robert Aldridge
George Michael Lanbinger	George Michael Lanbinger	. . . .
Andrew Freitley	Andrew Frietley	. . . .
Thomas Speak	Thomas Speak	. . . .

For Robert Ruther ford was Moses Lambert
For Col. John Hite – James Hoge Jr.
For Henry Brinker – Everhart Daring

69

BIBLIOGRAPHY

In the course of this study we have consulted the authorities which follow. These authorities are cited in parentheses, abbreviated as indicated, in the body of the account.

Anburey, Thomas: *Travels through the Interior Parts of America* - London, 1791 (*Anburey*)

Barnaby, Rev. Andrew: *Travels Through the Middle Settlements in North America* - London, MDCCLXV (*Barnaby*)

Brown, Stuart E., Jr.: *Virginia Baron* - Berryville, Va. 1965 (*Brown*)

Cartmell, T. K.: *A History of Frederick County, Virginia* - Winchester, 1909 (*Cartmell*)

Callahan, Charles M.: *George Washington, the Man and the Mason* - Washington 1913 (*Callahan*)

Fithian, Philip Vickers: *Journal 1775 - 1779* - Princeton 1934 (*Fithian*)

Fitzpatrick, John C.: *George Washington - Colonial Traveller* - Bobbs-Merrill 1927 (*Fitzpatrick*)

Freeman, Douglas S.: *Young Washington* - New York 1948 (*Freeman*)

Frederick County Deed Books: (*F.D.B.*)

Frederick County Order Books: (*F.O.B.*)

Greene, Katherine Glass: *Winchester, Virginia and Its Beginnings* - Strasburg 1926 (*Greene*)

Hamilton, S. M.: *Letters to Washington* - New York 1901 (*Hamilton*)

Hening, William W.: *Statutes at Large* - Richmond, 1809 (*Hening*)

Journal of the Virginia House of Burgesses (*Journal H. of B.*)

Kercheval, Samuel: *History of the Valley of Virginia* 4th Ed. Strasburg, 1925 (*Kercheval*)

Koontz, Louis K.: *The Virginia Frontier 1754 - 1763* - Hopkins Press, Baltimore, 1925 (*Koontz*)

Morton, Frederic: *The Story of Winchester in Virginia* - Strasburg, 1925 (*Morton*)

Proprietor's Grants to Lots in the Town of Winchester, Va. State Library (*Props. Grants*)

Quarles, Garland R.: *One Hundred Old Homes in Winchester* - Winchester, 1967 (*Quarles - Win. Homes*)

Russell, William G.: *What I Know about Winchester,* Winchester, 1953 (*Russell*)

Sargent, Winthrop: *History of the Expedition Against Fort Duquesne,* Philadelphia, 1856 (*Sargent*)

Sharpe, Horatio: *Correspondence* - Archives of Maryland (*Sharpe*)

Virginia Magazine of History and Biography. (*Va. Hist. Mag.*)

Washington, George - *Diaries* - Edited by Fitzpatrick, New York, (*Diaries*)

> *Writings* - Edited by Fitzpatrick, Washington, D.C. 1932 (*Writings*)

> *Account Book* - Manuscript Dept., Library of Congress

> *Papers* - Manuscript Dept., Library of Congress

Winchester Deed Books - (*W.D.B.*)

INDEX

72

Bradford, Charles 65.
Branson: John 66; Thomas 58.
Bridger, John 63.
Brinker, Henry 22, 49, 50, 68, 69.
Briscoe, John 47, 50, 64.
Brock, Henry 66.
Brooks, David 65.
Brounfield, Charles 62.
Brown: Isaac 60; John 63; James 44, 59;
    Samuel 59; Stewart 10.
Brubaker, Abraham 46, 63.
Bruce: George 51, 61; James 66.
Brucetown 15.
Bruin, Bryan 51, 68.
Buck, Charles 49, 51, 68.
Buckles, Robert 51.
Buckley, John 51.
Bull, Robert 61.
Bullit, Lt. Thomas 34.
Bullskin Creek (Area) 3, 8, 16, 42.
Burden: John 51; Joseph 50.
Burgesses, Va. House of 4, 9, 11, 13, 14,
    18, 20, 24, 28, 33, 35, 39, 43, 44, 50, 58.
Burgoyne, Gen. John 30.
Burk, Tobias 51, 60.
Burkhart, Reagart (?) 66.
Burn: James 50; William 46.
Burner, Jacob 50, 59.
Bush, Philip 36, 69.
Bush, Philip's Inn 43.
Butler: John 36; Thomas 47, 67.

C—

Caldwell, Andrew 44.
Calman, Matthew 51.
Calmes: Marquis 64; William 45, 51, 64.
Calvert: Richard 64; Robert 49.
Calvey, John 44.
Calvin (Colvin): Andrew 51; Joshua 51.
Campbell: Douglas 59; Henry 36; John
    35.
Cameron Street 33.
Capon Bridge 14.
Capon, Forks of 5.
Capon River 6.
Carlisle, Pa. 34, 41.
Carlyle, John 2, 40, 51.
Carney, Thomas 51, 68.
Carolina 38.
Carr, Nathaniel 51, 67.
Carson, Simon 51, 62.
Carter: James 49, 68; Henry 38, James
    Jr. 51; Thomas 67.
Cartmell (Cartmill): Edward 44, 66;
    Nathan 49; Nathaniel 38, 48, 67; Tho-
    mas K. 7, 8.
Cary, Col. 2.
Catawba Indians 30, 31, 37.

Cates Marsh 3.
Catlet (Catlett): James 64; Peter 64.
Caton, Thomas 51.
Chambers, William 66.
Chandler, Jacob 68.
Chaplin, William 51.
Charles Town, W. Va. 3, 15.
Christian, Jacob 47, 60.
Chenoweth (Chennowith): John 44, 51,
    62; Thomas 64; William 46, 65; Will-
    iam Jr. 65.
Cherokee Indians 31, 37, 38.
Chester: David 51, 68; Thomas 6, 45, 51.
City Hall (Winchester) 33.
Clark: Christopher 51; William 61.
Clarke County 6.
Clarke, Debora 2.
Clark's Gap 15.
Clearbrook 15.
Cloud: Henry 51; Jeremiah 44.
Cock (Cocks, Cox), Capt. William 11, 16,
    31, 32, 35, 51.
Cock House 31.
Cock Tavern 32.
Cockener (Gochenour), Jacob 51, 61.
Cochran, William 45, 51, 66.
Coddys (Caudy's Castle) 5.
Coil, William 51, 64.
Coleman's 15.
Colson: John 60; Thomas 49, 68.
Colston: John 51, Thomas 51.
Colvil (Colvin), James 65.
Colvin (Calvin, Colvil): Andrew 61;
    James 47; Joseph 47, 66.
Conegers (?), William 65.
Congress, Library of 25.
Conococheque 15.
Conrad: Frederick 68; Henry 62.
Conrad House 33.
Cook, John 51.
Cooper: Jacob 49; Leonard 67; Thomas
    51, 68.
Corder, Edward 51, 68.
Cordrey: Edward 48; Thomas 51.
Cork Street 7, 8, 9, 10.
Corlet, John 64.
Court House (Frederick) 9, 22, 36, 40.
Court House Barracks 33.
Cowper, Jacob 51.
Craik, Dr. James 37, 38, 51, 58.
Crawford: Valentine 44, 63; Valentine
    Jr. 51; William 49, 64.
Cresap's Plantation 5, 13, 15.
Crider (Grider): Frederick 48; Martin
    64.
Cromley: James 45, 51, 64; John 51, 64;
    William 51; William Jr. 62.
Cryler, Martin 51.
Culpeper County 5.

Cumberland, Md. 12, 13, 14, 15.
Cumberland Road 42.
Cunningham, Robert 45, 51, 66.

D—

Daring, Everhart 67, 69.
Dark, Joseph 65.
Daste, Abraham 61.
Datry (Dietrich), David 38.
Daugherty: Jarvis 48, 63; William 48, 63.
Davidson, Walter 68.
Davis: Edward 58; James 59; John 48, 65; William 44, 58.
Deadrick (Dietrich), David 36, 52, 67.
Denton: Abraham 63; Capt. John 45, 67; Samuel 45.
Deviney: George 59; Hugh 45.
Dick, Charles 51.
Dillon, William 48, 66.
Dillon's Run 6.
Dinwiddie, Gov. Robert 11, 12, 13, 14, 15, 17, 18, 23, 24, 26, 27, 30, 33, 34.
Dodd, Edward 45, 52, 61.
Dodson, John 68.
Doster, Thomas 44, 52, 66.
Dow, John 36, 52.
Dowdall, James Gamul 32.
Duckworth, William 52.
Dumfries 3.
Dunbar, Col. Thomas 15, 18.
Duncan, Patrick 52.
Dunham: Joseph 47; Patrick 48.
Dunkin, Mathew 66.
Dutch Baker 22.
Dutch Cowper 38.
Dyer, John 52, 58.

E—

Eagle, Tevalt 63.
Earnest, Henry 68.
Earle, Samuel 67.
Easton, Henry 52, 62.
East Indies 2.
Eaton, Thomas 66.
Edwards: Ignatius 23; Joseph Jr. 60; Josiah Jr. 52; Robert 46.
Edwards, Fort 14.
Ellis, Thomas 52, 67.
Elphenston (Helphinstine), Philip 62.
Ender, Earnest 58.
Engles, Melchior 45.
Enoch, Henry 18.
Erie, Lake 12.
Etrick, David 45.
Evans: Griffith 36; Isaac 46, 52, 61; John 44, 62; William 47, 52, 59.
Ewings, William 52, 67.

F—

Fairfax: Anne 2; Bryan 2; George William 2, 3, 5, 39, 40, 52; Henry 2; Hannah 2; Sarah 2; Thomas 6th Lord 1, 2, 3, 5, 7, 10, 17, 28, 31, 40, 52; William 1, 2, 3, 12, 21, 25, 26.
Fairfax County 2, 37, 39, 43.
Fairfax Lane 28.
Fairmont Avenue 14.
Farrar, George 52.
Faucet, (Fawcett), Richard 47.
Fauquier County 3.
Feawood, John 59.
Fetzer, George 67.
Feugates, Martin 47.
Fewel, John 49.
Fields, Lewis 53.
Fife, John 52, 59.
Findley, James 65.
Fithian, Rev. Philip Vickers 29.
Fitzhugh, Col. William 16.
Flemon, Alexander 65.
Fletcher: Peter 58; Richard 58.
Foley, Richard 52, 68.
Follis, George 62.
Fonkhouser (Funkhouser): Jacob 62; John 61.
Forbes, Gen. John 30, 41.
Forbes Expedition 42.
Foreman, Peter 65.
Forts: Bowman 19; Cumberland 25, 26, 37, 40, 41; Duquesne 17, 18, 29, 30, 41, 42; Edwards 14; Evans 15; Fry 19; George 11, 15; Helm 19; Le Boeuf 12; Loudoun 11, 24, 26, 27, 28, 29, 30, 31, 37, 38, 40, 41; Necessity 14; White 19.
Fossett (Fawcett): John 52; Joseph 52, 68; Richard 52.
Foster: Isaac 52, 64; Peter 45; William 59.
Frables, Henry 61.
Franklin, Benjamin 16, 34.
Franks, Mr. 38.
Frazer, John 37.
Frederick County 1, 2, 4, 5, 6, 9, 13, 17, 19, 21, 39, 40, 41, 42.
Frederick Springs 4.
Frederick Town 1, 3, 4, 5, 7.
Frederick, Md. 15, 16.
Fredericksburg 12, 18, 21, 24, 33, 36.
Freeman, Dr. Douglas S. 6, 39.
French, the 2, 11, 12, 12, 15, 17, 18, 19, 21, 30, 37, 42.
Frietley, Andrew 69.
Frost, William 47, 52, 64.
Frowman (Froman), Paul 52.
Fry: Abraham 46, 52, 61; Benjamin 52,

74

59; Jacob 52, 59; Joseph 48, 52; Col.
Joshua 13, 14; Samuel 52, 59.
Fulsom, Robert 46.
Funkhouser, John 45, 52.
Funk: Adam 47; Henry 52, 67; Capt.
John 52, 61; John Jr. 67; Joseph 52;
Martin 49, 52, 66; Matthias 48, 52, 66.

G—

Gaddes, William 44, 65.
Gatlet, James 45.
Genn, James 3, 5.
Gibson Jacob 47, 52, 64.
Giger, Jacob 63.
Glass: David 48, 52, 60; Joseph 47, 64;
Philip 46, 52, 58; Robert 44, 52, 63;
Samuel 67.
Glen: John 52, 61; William 66.
Glen Burnie 4.
Glover, William 67.
Golden Buck, The 36.
Gottlieb, Brother 4.
Gordon, Rev. John 47.
Grabill (Grable): Christian 47, 67; Chris-
topher 52; John 48, 61.
Graham's Magazine 41.
Grant, Frederick 65.
Great-Cape-Capon 18.
Greenfield (Greenafield), John 36, 37,
38, 66.
Greenway Court 10, 11.
Grider (Crider), Frederick 48.
Griffith, Edward 52, 61; John 65.
Grim, Charles 68.
Grinnan, John 52, 68.
Grogan, Thomas 66.
Grove, Matthias 60.
Grub, Benjamin 35, 45.

H—

Haddle (Handel), John 45.
Haines: Abraham 49; Hugh 60; Robert
53, 65.
Halfpenny, Robert 44, 53, 65.
Halifax County 18.
Halkett, Sir Peter 15, 18.
Hall, William 46, 65.
Hampshire County 6, 18, 40.
Hampton: George 47, 53, 60; Noah 52;
Thomas 44, 53, 60.
Hampton, Va. 2, 17.
Handley: Murtry 53, 59; Sichman 62.
Hanshaw, Nicholas 53, 63.
Handshires, Nicholas 47.
Hanger, Peter 60.
Harbinger, John 52.
Hardin: George 53; John 68.
Hardy County 6.

Harling, Moses 67.
Harner, Joseph 53, 60.
Harper, Robert 53, 65.
Harrison: Burr 59; Thomas 64.
Harrom, John 53.
Hart: Stephen 62; Thomas 53.
Harwich, Nicholas 62.
Hawkins, Williams 68.
Hayfield 14.
Heath, Dr. Henry 34.
Hedge: James 53; Jonah 58; Joshua 63.
Heintz, (Christian, Christopher) 37.
Heiskel, Christopher 68.
Helm (Helms): Leonard 44; Meredith
49; Thomas 49, 53; William 49, 53.
Helphinstine, Philip 62.
Helvestone (Helphinstine) 36.
Henry, George 47, 53, 62.
Heth, Henry 37, 46, 48, 53, 62.
Hewitt, Wm. N. 15.
Hiat (Hyatt): George 68; John 46; John
Jr. 46; William 62.
Higgins, Tim 35.
Highlanders, 77th Regiment 42.
Highland (Hiland), Richard 48, 53, 67.
Hill, Joseph 60.
Histant (?), Henry 44.
Hite: Isaac 53, 58; Jacob 53, 64; Col.
John 53, 59; John 62; Yost 3, 5, 32.
Hiver, Daniel 36.
Hobson, William 59.
Hockman, Christopher 61.
Hodgson, Robert 65.
Hoff, Lawrence 65.
Hoge (Hogg): George Jr. 59; James 44,
53, 59; James Jr. 53, 65, 69; Rev. John
53, 61; William 60.
Hogeland: John 66; Richard 58.
Holdman: Daniel 66; Jacob 64.
Holladay, James 66.
Holler, Peter 62.
Hollingsworth: George 49, 63; Isaac 49;
Zebulon 44.
Holman, Daniel 46.
Hood, Lunis 59.
Hopes (Hopes), John 49, 53, 58.
Hopewell Meeting House 15.
Horner, Joseph 44.
Hornsby, Leonard 66.
Hotzenbella: George 68; Stephen 53, 68.
Houghhacker, George 62.
Houghman (Hoffman, Huffman): Chris-
tian 46; Peter 46.
House, John 53.
Housman, John 53, 67.
Howels (Huddles), Charles 45.
Huddle (Hottle): Charles 64; George 47,
53.
Hultz, Josiah 66.

Humbert, Godfrey 36, 53, 65.
Hunter: Adam 45, 52; Col. John 34.
Hust, William 48.
Hyat, Simeon 53.

I—

Indians 11.
Indian Alley 31.
Indian Hollow Road 14.
Innes, Col. James 25.
Irish Regiments 15.
Isaacs: Elisha 60; Samuel 47, 53.

J—

Jackson & Fitzsimmons 37.
Jefferson, Peter 13.
Jefferson County 3, 6.
Jenkins: Aaron 46, 53; George 37, 62; John 59; Owen 36.
Jennings, Daniel 37.
Jones: Gabriel 37, 39, 40, 44, 53; John 53, 67; Joseph 53, 69; William 67.
Johnston: Daniel 45, 53; George 7, 8, 9; Stephen 65.
Jolliffe (Jolleffe): James 65; William 44; William Jr. 53.
Jordan, Peter 53, 63.

K—

Kackley, Jacob 68.
Keaner, Ulrich 60.
Keller, George 53, 62.
Kennedy: Alexander 36; Thomas 62.
Kennison, Kate 37.
Kerfert, William 65.
Kernstown 29.
Keys, Gersham 47, 66.
Keywood, John 53.
Kirkpatrick, Thomas 36.
Knave, Henry 67.
Knight, James 48, 53, 64.
Kockenal (Kuykendahl), Henry 47.
Koontz, Louis K. 19.
Kurtz: Adam 10; Johann Adam 9.
Kurtz House 11, 17, 32.

L—

Laubinger, George Michael 69.
Lambert: Christian 68; Moses 60, 69.
Langdon: Jonathan 59; Joseph 44, 59; Joshua 53.
Laren, Isaac 54, 60.
Larrack (Larrick), John 66.
Lee: George 2; Col. Henry 21.
Leith, John 54.
Lemley, John 32.
Lemon: James 49; John 45, 54, 67; Nicho-
las 44, 54; Robert 45, 63; Thomas 53.
Lemon's (Ordinary) 33.
Lewis: David 46, 62; Fielding 38, 58.
Leyden, Patrick 36.
Library of Congress 38.
Lilburn, Francis 54, 66.
Limback, John 47.
Linder: Lawrence 62; Simeon 48.
Lindsey (Lindsay): One 39; Edmund 54, 64; Edward 45; James 54; John 54; Thomas 48, 67.
Little Cacapon River 6, 13, 15.
Littler: John 60; Samuel 46, 53.
Littleton, Charles 60.
Lloyd: Henry 46, 54, 65; James 53, 60.
Lochmiller, George 54, 68.
Loudon, Thomas 54.
Long, William 66.
Long Marsh 3.
Longaggars (Longacres): Andrew 47, 53, 62; Edward 48.
Loudoun, Lord 20.
Lords of Trade 12.
Lorenger (Laubinger), George Michael 53.
Loudoun Street 11, 17, 29, 31, 32, 35.
Low, Thomas 48, 62.
Loyal Hannon 41.
Lucas: Edward 53, 59; Edward Jr. 65; Robert 59.
Lupton: John 61; Joseph 47, 53, 63; William 48, 53, 66.
Lyles, Hugh 45, 64.
Lyllbourn, Francis 47.

M—

Maddin (Madden): John 49, 68; Laughlin 54; Mayberry 54, 58.
Magill, James 60.
Main Street 31.
March, Michael 63.
Marney, Michael 63.
Marney, Robert 47, 54, 66.
Marr, Christopher 48.
Martin: Bryan 41; Thomas 65; Thomas Bryan 40, 50, 61.
Maryland 4.
Mason, Thomas 46, 54.
Matthews, Alexander 44.
Maurer, George 58.
Mayo River 18.
McCarty, Darby 54, 61.
McCormack (McCormick): James 64; John 45, 64; Joseph 54.
McCoy, Robert 49, 54, 66.
McDaniel, Patrick 54.
McDonald, Alexander 62.
McDowel (McDowell, McDowels): John 54; Joseph 45, 54.

76

McGill's 42.
McGill, James 44, 54.
McIntire, Nicholas 63.
McKee, William 45.
McKenny, George 60.
McKey, William 63.
McMachen: John 60; Richard 46, 67; William 59.
McMahan: Richard 54; William 54.
McNeal, Archibald 66.
Meldrum, Rev. William 54.
Mellan, Isaac 61.
Melon, David 46.
Mendinghall, John 47, 54.
Mendenhall (Mendinghall) Mills 42.
Mercer: Capt. 26; Edward 65; Edward Jr. 46, 54, 68; George 24, 43, 58; James 58; John 68; Moses 66; Richard 44, 54, 58.
Mercersmith, Henry 62.
Merchant, William 60.
Middleway 15.
Milburn: John 47, 54; Robert 54.
Miles, George 66.
Miller: David 54, 59; Jacob 54, 58, 60; William 46, 54, 58.
Mitchell, John 36.
Monger, William 54.
Monongahela River 12.
Moon, Jacob 47, 54, 59.
Moore: Henry 48, 54, 59; James 63; Lewis 54, 58; Reuben 60; Ryley 44; William 46.
Moravian Church 4.
Morgan: David 54, 68; Morgan 48, 54, 60, 68; Morgan Jr. 54; Richard 45, 54; Zachariah 68.
Morgan County 6.
Morris, James 58.
Moyer: Henry 58; John 65.
Mowrey, George 47.
Mt. Vernon 2, 5, 16, 18, 29.
Mungars, William 35, 36, 65.
Murphey: Darby 49, 54, 67; Michael 67.

N—

Naffe, John 46.
Nealy: John 62; William 44.
Neavil (Neville), George 3.
Neill, Lewis 65.
Newal, Samuel 61.
Neirl (?), George 54.
Neiskirk, Tunis 66.
Newkirk, Narnard 64.
Neitzell, Christian 38.
Newman: Samuel 64; Samuel Jr. 64; Walter 62.
Nicholas, George 66.

Night (Knight), James 48.
Nisewanger, John 48, 54.
North Carolina 13, 33.
North Mountain 42.
Northern Neck Grant 1, 2, 5.
Nottoway Indians 36, 37.

O—

Ogle, George 62.
Oglesby, Alexander 45, 60.
Ohio Company 12.
Ohio River 12.
Old Court House (Fairfax) 15.
Oldtown, Maryland 5, 13, 15.
Opequon Church 29.
Opequon Creek 15.
Oranamus (Hieronimous), Conrad 59.
Orme, Robert 16.
Osborn (Osbourne), David 44, 60.
Otto: 36; Tobias 65.
Oxford, England 13.

P—

Page County 6.
Painter, John 55, 67.
Palace Theater 35.
Parke, John 61.
Parkins (Perkins): Charles 49, 67; Elisha 47; Isaac 28, 37, 39, 44, 54.
Parks, Samuel 44.
Parrell: John 55, 62; Joseph 46, 55.
Patten, Samuel 47.
Patterson: John 38; William 54, 64.
Patton's Furniture Store 31.
Paul: Andrew 46; George 54; Robert 46, 65.
Paxton, Reuben 48, 62.
Pearce, Lewis 58, 59.
Pearis: Richard 61; Robert 44, 55.
Pearson, Samuel 47, 55, 68.
Peckering, William 55.
Pemberton: George 46, 55, 60; Isaac 47; Isiah 66; Josiah 55.
Pence: Lawrence 54; Lewis 59.
Pennington, Capt. Isaac 3.
Pennsylvania 41.
Pennywit, John 61.
Perkins (Parkins): Charles 54; Jonathan 55.
Perry: Joseph 36; Peter 55; Thomas 48, 55, 61.
Peters, Otho 47.
Petersburg, W. Va. 5.
Peugh (Pugh): Agariah 48; Jesse 48.
Peyton, Mrs. 29.
Philadelphia 18, 34, 38.
Philips, William 60.
Pickering, William 67.

77

Pierce, John 58.
Pifer, Harry 47.
Piger (?), Nicholas 63.
Pike, Henry 62.
Pitman, Anthony 61.
Pittsburg 29.
Plank, John 61.
Pleubert, Frederick 70.
Poker: George 63; Michael 54, 60; Philip 55, 69.
Postgate, Thomas 55.
Potomac River 4, 5, 6, 15, 16.
Potter, William 48.
Prince, John 65.
Prince William County 3.
Princeller, Nicholas 45, 54.
Pritchard: Reese 48; Samuel 55.
Pritchett, Reuben 44.
Providence Island 2.
Pugh: Azariah 55, 65; Jesse 55, 67; Job 55, 62; Joseph 68; Thomas 55, 58.
Pursols, Jacob 47.

Q—

Quebec, Siege of 2.

R—

Ramey, William 62.
Rangers 20.
Rankin: David 60; Henry 59; William 60.
Rayborn, Robert 44.
Raystown, Penna. 41.
Read, Edward 65.
Reapsoner (?), George 65.
Reece: Henry 55, 68; Jacob 47, 66; Morrice 63; Thomas 55, 67; Thomas Jr. 67.
Reed, John 48, 55.
Reeves, Morris 45.
Reid, John 66.
Reynolds (Reynalls, Rannels): Joseph 67; William 49, 55, 66.
Rhodes, John 59.
Rice: Edmund 61; George 55, 67; Patrick 47, 55, 62.
Riddell, Isaac 55.
Ridgeway, Josiah 68.
Rinker: Henry 38, 55, 68; Casper 67.
Road, John 55.
Roberts: Joseph 48, 55; Owen 59; William 45, 55, 66; William Jr. 45, 55.
Robinson: Edward 60; John 20, 33.
Rock Creek 15.
Rogers: Edward 55; Evan 66; Owen 48, 68; William 61.
Romney, West Va. 5.
Romney Road 14.
Ross: Alexander 62; George 46, 55, 58.
Royal Navy 2.

Ruble (Rubble): David 61; George 67; Peter 61; Ulrich 55.
Ruddle (Ruddles): Archibald 64; Carnel 55; Cornelius 62; George 63; Isaac 46.
Rufover, Peter 46.
Russell: William 47, 55, 59; William Greenway 29.
Rutherford: Benjamin 58; Robert 28, 32, 45, 55, 69; Thomas 10, 59.

S—

Sagey, Thomas 64.
Sample, Samuel 63.
Saratoga 30.
Sawyer, Samuel 61.
Scene, John 56.
Schrack, Nicholas 55.
Seabrat (Siebert, Seabright), Jacob 37, 56, 65.
Seaman, Jonas 55, 64.
Sellar, George 47, 61.
Seltzer, Matthew 62.
Sewell, John 56.
Shade, George 56.
Sharpe: Gov. Horatio 16; Thomas 56, 66; Zebulon 56.
Shearer, John 44, 62.
Shenandoah County 6.
Shenandoah River 3.
Shenandoah Valley 16.
Shephard (Shepherd): David 44; Thomas 56, 66.
Shepherdstown, Md. 16, 42.
Shibley: Daniel 61; Frederick 61.
Shippensburg, Pa. 41.
Shirley: Jarvis 67; Walter 60; Gov. William 18.
Shoemaker, George 61.
Shull, Peter 64.
Sibert, Bernard 46.
Skeen, John 48.
Small, John 46, 56.
Smallgolfer, Lawrence 55.
Smalsapper, Lawrence 67.
Smalthousen, Lewis 47.
Smith: Charles 27, 40, 41, 55, 68; Daniel 65; Jeremiah 46, 56, 68; John 28, 55, 60; William 23.
Snapp (Snap): John 46, 55, 58; John Jr. 45, 55, 58; Lawrence 56, 67.
Snickers, Edward 36, 56, 64.
Snider: George 63; Simon 64.
Snodgrass: David 55, 64; John 59, 61.
Somersetshire, England 13.
South Mountain 15, 16.
South Branch of Potomac 4, 5.
Southwood, Stephen 45.
Sowers, Jacob 22, 48, 55, 67.

78

Spain 2.
Speake, Thomas 56, 69.
Speary (Sperry), Peter 67.
Spottswood, Col. 33.
Spottsylvania County 33.
Springer: Dennis 49, 56; Josiah 67.
Spurgen, William 46.
St. Clair, Sir John 35.
St. Clair, Lake 15.
Stalker, Peter 37.
Stanwix, Col. John 20, 23, 24, 27.
Stephen, Adam 13, 24, 25, 35, 38, 43, 58.
Stephens: Daniel 56; Henry 47, 55, 63;
    Lawrence 44, 56, 62; Lewis 49, 56, 63;
    Peter 47, 55, 63.
Stephenson: Richard 45, 60, 56; William
    56.
Stephens City 29.
Sterly, Jacob 60.
Steward, Robert 67.
Stewart: Capt. 27; John 22; Robert 55,
    56; William 60.
Stickle, John 55.
Stine's Chapel 14.
Stinson, William 63.
Stockdon, Robert 48.
Stover, Ulrich 47, 55, 68.
Stonebridge, John 65.
Stover: Daniel 55; Jacob 56; Peter 47,
    56, 59.
Stribling, Taliaferro 45, 59.
Stricker, Moses 65.
Strickler: Benjamin 55; Jacob 55, 59;
    John 45, 59; Joseph 56, 59.
Strode, Jeremiah 60.
Stroop, William 45.
Strother's Lane 14.
Stroud: James 58; Jeremiah 48; John 56,
    64; Samuel 44.
Stroupe, William 63.
Stuart, Robert 66.
Sturman, Richard 66.
Sugarland Run 15.
Swan, Andrew 65.
Swearingen: Thomas 39, 40, 41, 44, 50,
    58; Van 42, 44, 44, 62.
Swearingen's Ferry 16.
Syler, Barnard 58.

T—

Tate, Magnus 44, 56, 58.
Taylor: Abraham 63; Harrison 49, 56, 67;
    Jonathan 67; John 56, 61; Samuel 56;
    Simeon 56, 66, 68; Thomas 65.
Teague, Edward 46.
Tewalt (Tevalt), John 46.
Tharp, Zebulon 63.
Thomas: Edward 48, 56, 60; Ellis 45, 56,

68; Enos 45, 59; Evan 45, 56, 60; John
    45, 48, 56, 59, 62; Owen 56, 63.
Thompson, Joseph 56, 60.
Thornbury: Benjamin 46, 63; Thomas 46.
Tipton, John 59.
Tomlinson, Benjamin 38.
Town Run 31, 33.
Town House 33.
Trent, Capt. 13.
Trinkle, Stephen 63.
Troutwine, George Isaac 68.
Turner: Anthony 46, 56, 59, 64; Anthony
    Jr. 46, 56.
Tyson's Corner 15.

V—

Vanbraam, Jacob 12.
Vance: Alexander 44, 56; Andrew 41, 56,
    63; David 44, 56, 58; James 56, 64;
    John 46, 56, 64; Joseph 56, 68; Samuel
    46, 56, 63, 65; William 56, 64.
Vanmeter: Abram 46, 56, 59; Henry 44,
    56, 62; Jacob 45, 56, 62, 63; John 56,
    58.
Vanfagan, John Frederick 56.
Vestal, John 47, 56, 68.
Vestals Gap 13, 15.
Virginia Baron 11.
Virginia, Governor and Council 9.
Virginia Militia 11.
Virginia Regiment 38.

W—

Wadlington, Thomas 48.
Walker, Sarah 2.
Walton, Moses 66.
Wappacomo Road 14.
Warren County 6.
Washington: Charles 58; John 58; John
    Augustine 17, 32; Lawrence 2, 12;
    Samuel 58.
Washington's Account Book 17, 32.
Washington's Headquarters 7, 8, 11.
Washington's Office 7, 9, 10, 11.
Washington Slept Here 43.
Watson, Dr. 36, 38.
Watkins: David 64; John 62; Thomas 57.
Weaver, George 63.
Wendall: August 57; Christian 57; Valen-
    tine 57.
West, Hugh 39, 40, 41, 44, 50.
West Virginia 6.
Whitacre 13, 15.
White: Isaac 57, 65; John 44; Joseph 59;
    Robert 66; William 48, 57, 59; William
    Jr. 59.
Whitzel, George 57.
Winchester 4, 9, 12, 13, 14, 16, 18, 19, 20,

79

21, 24, 25, 26 28, 30, 32, 35, 37, 41, 42, 43.

Winchester City Council 7.

Windle (Windles): Augustine 49, 64; Christian 62; Christopher 47; Valentine 48, 64.

Winkfield, Owen 61.

William and Mary College 5, 13.

Williamsburg 14, 15, 28.

Williamsport, Md. 15.

Wilkerson, Joseph 49. 57.

Wills Creek 12, 13, 14, 15, 16, 17.

Wilson: Edward 59; James 57, 60; John 57, 63, 67; Robert 57, 58, 63; Robert Jr. 63; Thomas 59; William 57.

Withers, Ralph 48, 57.

Wood: Col. James 4, 9, 10, 11, 21, 28, 33, 40, 41, 47, 56, 58; Mary 10, 28; Thomas 35.

Wood's Addition 10.

Woolf (Wolfe): Jacob 60; Michael 59; Peter 46, 57, 63.

Woodrow, Alexander 56, 64.

Worth, Robert 57, 68.

Worthington: Robert 49, 57, 64; Robert Jr. 49; Samuel 65; Thomas 37.

Wright (Right): David 48, 57, 64; George 35, 57, 64; Isaac 64; Jacob 57, 60; James 57; John 57, 68; Thomas 61; William 63.

Y—

Yorkshire, England 2.
Young, John 57.